Praise for *The Release*

Whenever I have lost my way as a writer, Elizabeth Jarrett Andrew arrives as a trusted companion. Whether I'm drafting new material, revising, or sending my work out in the world, I can always find just the right words I need to hear in Andrew's books. I've recommended her writing guides to countless students in my two decades as a creative writing professor, and always they respond with immense gratitude for her insights.

—Brenda Miller, author of *Tell it Slant: Creating, Refining, and Publishing Creative Nonfiction* and *The Pen and the Bell: Mindful Writing in a Busy World*

I'm a major fan of this book and believe it will offer sustenance, guidance, relief, challenge, a healthier way forward, and a route to healing for many writers. This was the book I needed so long ago and the book that can change my trajectory.

—Mona Susan Power, author of *Council of Dolls* and *Grass Dancer*

Elizabeth Jarrett Andrew is not only an author you should read but a teacher you can trust.

—Barbara Brown Taylor, author of *An Altar in the World* and *Leaving Church*

This book is like a wise friend—it energized me to think more broadly about what my work is in my life and in my relationships, and it expanded my thinking around the unexpected ways that my writing can interact with the wider world.

—Annika Martin, *New York Times* bestselling author

The Release gave me a much broader and more loving way to approach publishing.

—Carolyn Holbrook, author of *Tell Me Your Names* and *I Will Testify*

The Release

Creativity & Freedom After the Writing Is Done

Elizabeth Jarrett Andrew

Skinner House Books
Boston

Copyright © 2024 by Elizabeth Jarrett Andrew. All rights reserved. Published by Skinner House Books, an imprint of the Unitarian Universalist Association, 24 Farnsworth St., Boston, MA 02210–1409.

www.skinnerhouse.org

Printed in the United States

Cover design by Carol Chu
Author photo by Emily Jarrett Hughes

print ISBN: 978-1-55896-928-5
eBook ISBN: 978-1-55896-929-2
Audiobook ISBN: 978-1-55896-932-2

6 5 4 3 2 1
29 28 27 26 25 24

Library of Congress Cataloging-in-Publication Data

Names: Andrew, Elizabeth, 1969- author.
Title: The release : creativity and freedom after the writing is done / Elizabeth Jarrett Andrew.
Description: Boston : Skinner House Books, 2024. | Summary: "A resource for writers to help reimagine the relationship between writer and completed writing"-- Provided by publisher.
Identifiers: LCCN 2024005946 (print) | LCCN 2024005947 (ebook) | ISBN 9781558969285 (trade paperback) | ISBN 9781558969292 (ebook)
Subjects: LCSH: Authorship--Psychological aspects | Authorship--Philosophy. | Authorship--Vocational guidance.
Classification: LCC PN171.P83 A53 2024 (print) | LCC PN171.P83 (ebook) | DDC 808.02--dc23/eng/20240708
LC record available at https://lccn.loc.gov/2024005946
LC ebook record available at https://lccn.loc.gov/2024005947

"Self-Publishing" © Arona Fay Roshal, reprinted by permission.

To the many writers who've so openly
shared their experiences with me, and to the
source of inspiration moving in us all.

Contents

Introduction

Why do I write? Writing helps me listen, expands my sense of what's possible, transforms me from the inside out. I believe *I'm writing a story* when, really, the story is writing me. I love writing because the act loves me into being.

What do I dislike about writing? The stage after I'm done when I have to figure out what to do with my manuscript, then do it. The looming moment when I come face-to-face with an audience. The consequent exhaustion, overwhelm, disappointment, rejection, straining, striving, jealousy, shame, feeling unseen, despair, and self-doubt. Sure, there are joyful moments when I find a publisher, celebrate a release, or receive a reader's praise, but having traversed this period post-completion often, I'm also wary of these successes because they occasionally knock me off of an otherwise healthy path. For years I treated the work of seeking and navigating publication like scrubbing the toilet. Much as I disliked the chore, doing it regularly I considered good writing hygiene.

Then, a few years ago, I took a few blithe publishing missteps that quickly plunged me into trouble. I made choices (about how I communicated my novel's focus to my agent, what I agreed upon with my publisher, and how I marketed the book) that made me feel dirty. I wound up at the doctor's office for heart palpitations and on the therapist's couch for anxiety and addictive behaviors. Once I cleaned up the mess, I swore never, ever, to lose myself like that again.

My mistake was not that I'd chosen to publish. Sharing creative work can be tremendous—a chance to connect with others, to grow, to widen our world. No, I stumbled when I'd allowed my own values to be subsumed by the market's. Once I stepped off a life-giving path, the consequences avalanched. I hadn't realized publishing could jeopardize my integrity.

Afterward I swore I'd never make that mistake again. For me, writing is first and foremost a practice of transformation. I'm committed to making artful literature, as best I'm able, but it seems to me that literature is only artful when it truthfully and effectively uplifts the human spirit, mine included, and that the *way* we writers offer our work to others should also follow this path. Surely I don't have to lose my bearings to launch a novel!

I believe creative endeavors have their own life, and part of my responsibility as a writer is to serve that life in the world. Often, although not always, that means sharing it. Before I loved writing, I first loved reading, how I assumed I was *reading a story* when really the story was reading *me*, changing me, until on closing the covers I woke to the world made new. When my writing ushers readers through this remarkable phenomenon, the creative cycle reaches completion. My work arrives. I believe what is born in solitude reaches fulfillment in relationship. Just because the tasks required to send my work into the minds and hearts of readers go against my grain, I'm not absolved from finishing the labor of creation. It's my responsibility to support the continuation of what I've made as it evolves into others' hearts and imaginations.

So I posited these questions: Must I be fettered to the whims of my ego and the market economy as I share my work? Or can I continue to be generative and free? Is it possible to approach the period after finishing as an opportunity for continued creativity—perhaps even an integral part of the writing process? What might it look like to stay grounded—

heck, even flourish—during this final stage? My answers have become this guidebook. Today, after I finish a project, I use the principles and exercises here to keep myself on a healthy path.

I'm not alone in this struggle. While writers are taught to believe that publication is the happily-ever-after ending to our efforts, this fairy tale almost never comes true. I know many people who can't even begin writing or lose steam mid-draft because they dread the hard work of reaching an audience, or because they perceive not publishing as failure. When I asked a dear friend why she wasn't writing, she answered, "But what would I *do* with it?" With no reliable, productive outcome, she aborted the entire process. I know writers who deny their desire to publish out of spiritual pretense or crushing fear. I've watched exceptional writers who dearly want to publish permanently shelve complete manuscripts after getting stymied by self-doubt or bogged down in the submission process. I've seen writers compromise themselves or their projects to get their work in print. And I've seen many writers successfully publish only to then self-destruct. Depression, anxiety, insecurity—these are common but rarely expressed responses to publication.

A great many manuscripts are rushed into the marketplace to satisfy the writer's ego needs or the publisher's profit wants. Writers who choose deliberately, with clarity and grace, *not* to publish are rare; most unpublished manuscripts are accompanied by disappointment, anger, and self-deprecation. Published writers who navigate the industry with integrity, staying faithful to the source of their inspiration and serving the essence of their stories, who understand revising, editing, and marketing as arenas for personal transformation or as acts of service—they exist, but their fierce interior conviction is quiet. Good models are hard to find. The public arena is crowded with attention-grabbers.

No matter which direction we choose, the terrain post-completion is riddled with land mines.

So I offer this guide to writers in hopes that we all might be spared some grief. The process I outline here, which I call "the release," helps us form the habits of mind, heart, and body that support our project's final flourishing and keep us creatively engaged. This practice isn't for everyone, nor is it for every project. It's for those so compelled that we write without guarantee of pay or audience. It's for those who write in response to the demands of our hearts, who are open to the work of spiritual transformation and committed to serving the life of our creative projects, who want to thrive as we journey into publishing, or not publishing, or whatever transpires after the writing is done. It is for finished pieces whose inner flame still burns.

We writers want to see quantifiable results from our efforts. We seek evidence that our art matters, that *we* matter. Yet how we envision these "results" and define "mattering" are influenced by a product-oriented culture dominated by privileged white men, discriminatory toward other genders and people of color, benefiting rationalism and consumerism, driven by scarcity, and fiercely competitive. I hope the guidance here lifts our heads out of the sandbox this culture insists we fight in and offers an alternative way to play. The perspectives I turn to for support are Indigenous, women-centered, queer, process-oriented, and informed by evolutionary theory and quantum physics. I lean heavily on research about and first-hand experiences of traditional gift economies, especially how they apply to artists, and on Christianity's mystical lineage, which posits receiving and giving as mutual gestures in a holy, relational dance. From these sources, and continuing the work I've done in *Writing the Sacred Journey* and *Living Revision: A Writer's Craft as Spiritual Practice,* I trace how a life-affirming creative practice can continue through the decisions and tasks we undertake once the writing is finished. Anyone—amateurs and professionals alike, those who intend to publish and those who do not, those with book length manuscripts and those with haiku written on the backs of envelopes—can do this practice. I address writers who have fully developed work in hand; however, those who have not yet begun or are mid-draft will find that an introduction to this practice shifts how they think about the end-stage, which then affects how they write. If we change the ship's destination, we have to trim the sails.

While writers are the artists I know best, I believe the principles of this practice apply to all art making. The terms *writing* and *story* I conceive of broadly to signify any artistic creation in hopes that these pages accommodate makers of all stripes. When we create with sincerity and affection, we swim in a transformational current that began long before we started and will continue far beyond completion. This guidebook is for anyone who wants to release their work with love.

Those of us who relish how the creative process brings us alive commonly assume that, when we're done, the glorious experience of co-creative emergence is over. Our pages are a final "product," without agency until they meet a reader. I posit here that, quite to the contrary, the life force pulsing within completed work is more influential than we assume and can move into ever-wider spheres regardless of publication. Not only that; we writers can also know unexpected, energizing, and wildly influential creativity post-completion. We can be free from the burden of seeking validation and measuring worth. We can make conscious choices that support our well-being, serve readers, tend our communities, and nourish the planet. I share these pages in hopes that the love we've given our creative work might be amplified by its release.

Part I:
Setting Intention

Before writers "make an offering to the world," it is their job "to clarify and hone their own contribution to the wider conversation." The first step in breaking out is actually taking the time to turn inward and look within.

—Tess Taylor quoting Kima Jones,
"The Art of Publicity"

The choices we make in love and for love co-create our future. When we see ourselves as part of the larger whole, we act on behalf of the whole of which we are a part. . . . We need a new way of being in the world that broadens diversity, deepens interiority and strengthens relationality.

—Ilia Delio,
The Unbearable Wholeness of Being

1   Creativity During the Release

Your writing projects are your babies. Sometimes you dream about them before conception; sometimes they emerge in a passionate rush. You raise them with care, patience, frustration, labor, and abiding joy. Like child-rearing, revision is long, arduous, and meaningful. Often it seems the kid will never grow up.

Then your baby is grown. The project is complete—more or less. It is *of* you but is decidedly *not* you because it has an essence, a unique identity. You've given it test runs with readers, so you know it stands on its own. You love it dearly, but like any parent sending a teenager off to school or cutting a twenty-something loose from the purse strings, you show that love best by releasing it.

Comparing writing to child-rearing (which, as a mother, I'm qualified to do) has helped me see that the mistakes I've made launching work have sprung from one incorrect assumption: I thought creativity ended when the project was finished. But now I see three distinct stages in the creative process. In the first stage, we generate; in the second, we revise; in the third, we release. The release begins with the completion of a project and ends when the artist is no longer actively involved with that project, which might be in a year or two or never. Once your child is a full-fledged adult, your responsibilities decrease significantly while your love continues and, ideally, grows. The release is that period in which you parent your adult project.

The release is radically different from earlier stages of writing but shares continuity with them. I see these stages like primary colors on a color wheel, each using a particular process with a distinct purpose while blending with its neighbors. Just as drafting includes making changes and imagining an audience, just as revision includes both generating and considering readers, the release includes solitary exploration and revision. The project enters a new state: It's done. In this new phase we need a new approach, one whose main gesture is not generating nor developing but sharing. We need to learn a new language to talk about marketing, its rhythm and syntax determined by generous consideration of the recipient. Once again, we must open our hearts to inspiration, however it arises.

Unlike other art forms in which collaborative interaction *is* the creative process (think improvisational theater or collectively developed dance performances or a jazz trio riffing on a theme), most writers compose alone. Eventually we reach out to others; as Stephen King advises in *On Writing*, "Write with the door closed; rewrite with the door open." I open that door slowly, first inviting in thoughts about potential readers and eventually test-driving my work with living readers. When I finish, I nurture the connections between my project and others by directing my energy toward interactions, collaborations, and sometimes contractual agreements. Regardless of how solitary or peopled your process has been, the release stage is definitively relational. Part ministry, part business, at its core the release is a creative process within a network of relationships.

Essentially our work during the release is to share the story's essence, its life force, with others. We can do this by obvious means, passing along the text. But that essence also resides inside of our bodies, so we can release our work subtly with our very being. Publishing, while it often augments a work's influence, is not necessary for an effective release. And for those who *do* want or need to publish, the hidden dimensions of sharing that life force, through our presence, relationships, and personal choices, are critical to releasing well.

Now when I finish a piece, I'm aware that two vessels carry the spark I so want to pass into the world: my words and myself. The release is the stage when we writers share the soul of our project—its gift.

2   Hazards During the Release

Most writers experience moments of growth, satisfaction, and connection even as we mindlessly blunder our way through the release. Essays I've chosen not to publish have become fodder for new work. When I published my first book, I didn't know what to expect, so every invitation to speak was a delight. When readers tell me how my blogposts affect them, I am profoundly grateful. The mistakes I made when launching my novel drive these pages. The gifts come, regardless.

But so does angst about my worthiness, inflated pride, a desperate need for recognition, humiliation at the plentiful rejections, frustration at the impenetrability of the publishing industry, exhaustion from trying so hard, disappointment when published work gets no attention, and despair of ever making a difference. Putting down the pen or printing up a final manuscript, I'm elated: *I did this!* But I also feel vacuous dread about whatever is next, or overwhelm, or grief. When I consider the joys I've known during the release, all of them have an unexpected, generative quality: Something new is born. When I examine the pitfalls, they share the dictates of one strong misconception: My project is "done" and therefore the creative process is over.

If we assume the creative evolution of a project is finished, a cascade of consequences follows:

- We tend to stop playing, experimenting, listening, and responding to that project.

- When we're not creative, we close ourselves to possibility. The project is no longer an agent of growth. We stop participating in the practices (experimenting, risk-taking, question-asking) that make us receptive to change.

- This limits our freedom. We assume the only paths available are "publish or perish," "share or don't." We frame our options dualistically. We accept the constraints of cultural norms.

- If we choose not to share finished work, we imagine there's nothing more to do or learn. So we move on. We're prone to equating unshared work with aborted creativity. We assume nothing comes of it.

- If we choose to share, we rarely understand the tasks as opportunities to grow—to be created and to participate in who we're becoming.

- If we choose to publish, the writing becomes a product. In a market economy, products are bought and sold. Our creative work becomes a commodity.

- We often identify with this product. Because we've put time, energy, and love into its making, we feel as if what we've created is an extension or proxy of our being. We hitch our sense of self and worth to its reception, our own success and failure entangled with the work's.

- Our definitions of success and failure are often determined by popular cultural norms. We miss an opportunity to imagine alternatives or to root our conception of success and failure in our own values.

- We have a propensity to grow attached to particular outcomes. When these outcomes come about, our ego inflates—we imagine we earned or caused the results. When these outcomes don't happen, our ego crashes—we imagine we weren't good enough or didn't work hard enough, or we decide the system treated us unfairly. While it may be true that we worked hard or not hard enough, were deserving or not deserving, or experienced discrimination, none of these outcomes are the final story. Nonetheless, we tend to assume they are.

- Because "success" is rare and "failure" common, we frame the world competitively. We adopt a scarcity mindset, perceiving rewards (publishing, grants, residencies, "likes," reviews, etc.) as few and writers in a mad clamber to secure them. This pits us against the only people who might provide companionship through this process—our colleagues.

- Without a creative practice, we lose our spiritual practice. With our sights trained on outcomes, we forget to enjoy, and be transformed by, the journey.

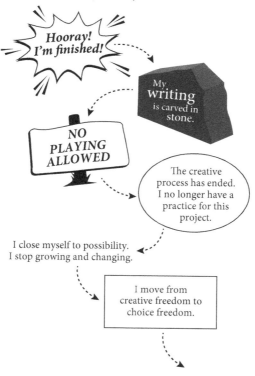

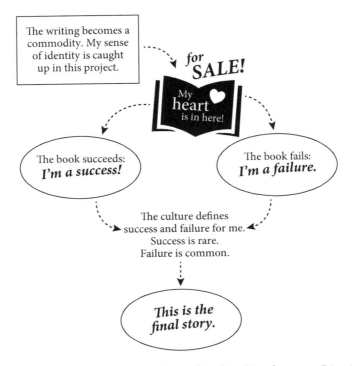

The writing becomes a commodity. My sense of identity is caught up in this project.

for SALE!

My heart ♥ is in here!

The book succeeds: *I'm a success!*

The book fails: *I'm a failure.*

The culture defines success and failure for me. Success is rare. Failure is common.

This is the final story.

Rather than careening down this familiar freeway, I invite you to rewind time. Go back to that period before your project was even a glimmer in your eye. How was it set in motion? When and how did you begin? Why? What were your expectations? What spurred you to stick with it through the rough spells? Is there any common denominator to these answers—any single, core instigation?

I believe the pilot light burning at the base of every creative project is longing. The nature of this longing differs for each of us and for every project, but generally we long for creative expression and relational fulfillment—to hear and be heard; to know and be known; to communicate; to arrive, to find wholeness and healing; to change and be changed; to explore, experiment, play, and thereby richly *live*; to *matter*; for our endeavors to matter. These longings metamorphize throughout the developmental stages until we face them head-on at completion, when we expect they will, at long last, be satisfied.

They won't. Or rather, they might be, but only in part, and the satisfaction will be short-lived.

When I think about my typical scramble to publish, I see myself grasping for connection. I want this bit of beauty I've forged from my most hidden being to commune with another's inner being, enlivening us both. There's continuity between the longing that got me writing and the longing that compels me to share my writing.

On the ground, though, my grasping isn't pretty. I imagine that getting the grant, landing the agent, or receiving hundreds of online reviews will signal I've arrived. *If only I get_____, I think, I'll be content.*

Sadly, the exhilaration we feel on finishing a project too often crashes into what Charles Salzberg called "postwritum depression." We've left behind the encompassing, cherished world we've engendered as well as our established patterns for entering it. If we're fortunate enough to publish, our initial elation is frequently followed by insecurity and emptiness. After memoirist Jessica Berger Gross's euphoric book launch and tour, she reflected, "I felt despondent. Rudderless. Tired. Inexplicably, I felt like a failure. Rather than feeling gratitude for what had happened, I obsessed over what hadn't. I judged myself for the brass rings I hadn't grabbed." She titled her essay about this disappointment, "I Just Published a Book: Why Am I Depressed?" I remember Mark Doty describing the high of receiving an NEA grant followed by three days of punishing self-doubt. Harper Lee was a hundred pages into her next novel when the success of *To Kill a Mockingbird* disrupted her permanently. "When you're at the top," she told her cousin, "there's only one way to go." For an up-and-coming author, the blessing of a multi-book contract becomes a curse as soon as the weighty expectations of publisher and public enter the writing studio. As musician and performance artist Amanda

Palmer says in *The Art of Asking*, "Outside approval can make The Fraud Police louder: it's more like fighting them in high court instead of in a back alley with your fists."

The trouble is, no external results will quench our longing. No one can validate our creative efforts. No kudos can assure us we've "arrived." Martha Graham biographer Agnes de Mille tells of a conversation that's worth relating here. Herself a choreographer, De Mille was dispirited; she believed her best work had been ignored by critics while her work on *Oklahoma!*, which she felt was only "fairly good," was a "flamboyant" success. De Mille told Graham that she saw only her work's "ineptitude, inorganic flaws, and crudities." "I am not pleased or satisfied," she said.

"No artist is pleased," Graham retorted.

"But then there is no satisfaction?"

"No satisfaction whatever at any time," Graham said. "There is only a queer divine dissatisfaction, a blessed unrest that keeps us marching and makes us more alive than the others."

Nothing—not publication, not great sales numbers, not stature, not being able to pay the bills, not even readers' gratitude or public conversations with presidents or being anthologized—will make this "queer divine dissatisfaction," this "blessed unrest," go away. Why? Because creative longing is a fundamental part of (I'd

creativity keeps the world alive, yet, everyday, we are asked to be ashamed of honoring it, wanting to live our lives as artists. i've carried the shame of being a "creative" since I came to the planet, have been asked to be something different, more, less, my whole life. thank spirit, my wisdom is deeper than my shame, and i listened to who i was. i want to say to all the creatives who have been taught to believe who you are is not enough for this world, taught that a life of art will amount to nothing, know that who we are, and what we do is life, when we create, we are creating the world. remember this, and commit.

—NAYYIRAH WAHEED,
SALT

argue) *everyone's* humanity. It is right and good. It fuels us. It urges us to seek union. At its core, this longing is holy. Only when we attach it to specific outcomes does it become destructive.

There will be no ultimate validation of our creative efforts, no conclusive satisfaction. When we enter the release looking to satiate our longing, we tilt at windmills. "The only real cure for post book depression?" writes Berger Gross; "Start writing something new." Creative fulfillment comes from creative engagement. That's it. Gandhi is reported to have said, "There is no way to peace. Peace is the way." For artists, creativity is our means and our ends.

We have to take the worthiness of our labor on faith. Faith for writers means holding dear the artistic impulse, interior liberty, and inventive agency—protecting, cultivating, and believing in these above all else. When writers say, "Trust the process," this is what we mean. Lan Samantha Chang offers this impassioned advice in a piece for *Lit Hub* called "Writers, Protect Your Inner Life":

> Hold onto that part of you that first compelled you to start writing. Hold onto that self through the vicissitudes of "career." A writing life and a writing career are two separate things, and it's crucial to keep the first. The single essential survival skill for anybody interested in creating art is to learn to defend this inner life from the world. Cherish yourself and wall off an interior room where you're allowed to forget your published life as a writer. Breathe deeply. Inside this walled-off room, time is different—it is flexible, malleable. We're allowed to bend it, to speed it up, slow it down, to jump forwards and backwards, as our minds do. We can circle back to our thoughts and memories picking and

choosing the most meaningful to us. There's a hushed, glowing sound, like the sound coming from the inside of a shell.

Faith like this only comes with practice, and the practice itself—more than the product—is where true value lies. Creative fulfillment is available to everyone, anyone, and the key is a loving practice.

3   Learning the Hard Way

Great intentions alone aren't enough to keep our feet to the fire and hearts flung wide during the release. There are simply too many insidious forces, both internally and externally, working to thwart us.

Embarrassing as it is, I'd like to offer my own crash-and-burn story by way of illustration. It's also a hopeful story because it shows how what we perceive as failure can, with intention and practice, bear gifts.

The First Wrong Turn

By my mid-forties, I'd written four books. The first, *Swinging on the Garden Gate,* was a memoir published by the Unitarian Universalist press, Skinner House Books; it sold about 1,500 copies before it went out of print. *On the Threshold*, a collection of personal essays, was accepted by an editor at a reputable midlist press who promptly lost her job when the press was bought by a large conglomerate; while the publisher released the book, their focus had shifted and my book no longer fit their list. *On the Threshold* was nominated for but did not receive a Minnesota Book Award and went out of print shortly afterward. *Writing the Sacred Journey: The Art and Practice of Spiritual Memoir* was also published by Skinner House and sales had slowly but steadily increased for a decade. A larger press would have remaindered it.

I had given a decade to writing my next book, a novel. Those years of learning a new genre were both arduous and fun. I relished fiction's freedom, the stimulation of research, the access the project gave me to intimate moments in others' lives, and the shockingly personal insights the process kicked up. Unlike the relatively tame events in my creative nonfiction, my character's life was physical, demanding, and dangerous, and it ignited my curiosity. I sensed that I was charting the final frontiers of women's rights and illuminating often overlooked dimensions of women's wisdom. I'd stumbled on an ideal topic to pursue my perennial questions: What does it mean to be an embodied spirit? How do we come alive?

To me, the novel was about faith grounded in experience and beyond the bounds of organized religion. I wrote for the sake of the story, and the story prospered. My budding delight in that formative process eventually led me to write *Living Revision*, in which I reframed the developmental stage of writing as a spiritual practice.

I desperately wanted the novel to catapult me out of obscurity into the literary arena. I don't think this aspiration colored the writing much—I'm pretty good at defending my inner liberty—but once the novel was done, ambition flooded in. I wanted an agent who could sell it to a major press. I wanted to continue "serving the story" by making a splash.

I was lucky; an agent I'll call Kathy agreed to represent the novel. I liked her a lot. Even though she mostly sold children's books, she was a proponent of women's issues and thought I'd written a great story. I knew she was excellent when she sent me twenty-seven single-spaced pages of revision suggestions, all of which improved the book. For four years she doggedly tried to sell it. Together we reworked the novel three times.

To no avail. I don't know why selling it was so difficult. Perhaps Kathy, because she lives on the west coast, didn't have the right New York contacts. Perhaps she didn't know the adult fiction market well enough. More likely the book wasn't up to snuff or the subject matter wasn't in vogue. Kathy was a persistent advocate; her years of effort never received adequate compensation. I remain deeply grateful to her.

In hindsight, however, I now see that the way I framed my novel in my query to her, and thus the reason Kathy took on my book, was perhaps the first of many missteps. From the get-go, I presumed (rightly or wrongly, I don't know) that agents who represent books about faith wouldn't have my literary standards or tolerate my out-of-bounds questions. I also assumed that mainstream literary agents would not represent a novel about faith, albeit a radical one. I hid the book's heartbeat—the central, undercurrent exploration that was its whole *raison d'être*—and presented it as a book about superficial aspects of the plot. The politics swirling around the subject were occasionally in the news and so to some extent a hot topic with an easy target audience, whereas readers drawn to the story's deeper exploration were harder to find, the subject a tougher sell.

I didn't lie to Kathy; any astute reader would see this thematic exploration. But I didn't position the book this way in my query, nor did I ever discuss this theme with Kathy, nor did she mention it in her pitch. This evasion, I believed, would serve the story by getting the novel further into the market than it might go otherwise. The ends would justify the means. I wanted success, and I believed the book's soul, should it be known, would sabotage that possibility.

As a result, Kathy tried to sell a different book from the one I had written. The book stopped becoming what it most wanted to become, and other forces took over.

The Second Wrong Turn

Kathy doggedly pitched the novel to publishers. After four years of ticking down our list, she informed me the next batch of pitches would be our last. We received the forty-eighth rejection, the forty-ninth . . . and then a publisher I'll call Smith nibbled. I couldn't remember how he'd gotten on the list. At the eleventh hour, the fiftieth pitch, we had an offer.

I took the call in my office, sitting on the edge of my chair. "It's a great book," Smith told me. "We think it's perfect for our women's list." I flinched at hearing once again the publishing industry's easy pigeonholes. The ensuing conversation I must leave to your imagination, but over its course, my spirits sank precipitously. I felt sick to my stomach. My every cell vibrated with dismay. On my bike ride home, tears streaked my face. I hated being a desperate author throwing herself at an unyielding publishing wall only to arrive at this miserable breakthrough, and I hated myself because I knew I would sign the contract. For the sake of the story, I'd sell out.

Secretly I felt that, if I didn't sign on with Smith, the novel would go unpublished or I'd have to self-publish, both of which I equated with failure. Ten years of work, I assumed, would be for naught. My passion for the subject would go nowhere; my devotion would prove fruitless and therefore meaningless. The literary world, within which I taught, would scorn me. I wanted to show my students I was worthy of their respect—a motivation so secret I barely saw it.

My intuition about Smith was spot-on. That I need to withhold the details is a sign of just how bad things got and how difficult it is to communicate to new writers the full array of publishing hazards. Suffice it to say my unwillingness to back out of the contract left me powerless. I ended our every interaction trembling. Thank goodness I never met the man in person. Without an editorial filter I trusted or a cover design I could stomach, the book's release terrified me. I spent hours raging, then weeping on my wife's shoulder. During the year and a half Smith and I worked together, my nerves grew increasingly frayed.

Disastrous as that publishing relationship was, I now own my responsibility in the matter. Really, what was more important, publishing success or my well-being? My prejudices against self-publishing proved unfounded, hurtful even. Remaining unpublished was a dignified choice I should have considered. My unexamined ambition tripped me mightily. By denying the novel's essence in the publication process, I quickly found my own essence compromised.

The Third Wrong Turn

Given Smith's limitations, I did my best; I hired my own copy editor and cover designer, I marketed with a vengeance. I made twenty pages of to-do lists—readings, reviewers, notices to alumni magazines, contest submissions, Facebook ads, online book clubs—and then drove myself to exhaustion doing them all. I strained for readers. In today's marketplace, I told myself, books are *made* successful, with effort and money. I didn't have the money, but I'd give the novel my effort. I would get the book into the hands of readers, and once the right people found it, it would take off.

I found myself hawking my book at professional conferences way outside my comfort zone, feeling fraudulent for only having imagined my way into their midst. I spoke at charming independent bookstores to clusters of three or five readers who invariably held the same job as my main character. I visited book groups where the discussion was hijacked by participants' personal stories. Glad as I was that my novel spurred women to share memories that otherwise remained secret, I would grow quiet, wondering why everyone seemed to have read a different book from the one I'd written.

The whole thing made me ill. I had heart palpitations. I felt trapped. I put myself into therapy because I knew something was wrong.

I applied to BookBub, an online marketing tool for indie writers; the novel was accepted. I paid the $500 fee, Smith reduced the ebook price to $0.99, and BookBub sent out its blast. Within twenty-four hours, it rose on the Amazon charts, making it to number six in literary fiction, compensating me for my expense plus some and rushing me with adrenaline. After that, I checked the ranking incessantly, wanting something more from it that I never found. When the ranking began to fall, my heart fell too. So I tried a different marketing tool or a Facebook ad or anything that might get those numbers up again. I read every Amazon or Goodreads review as though it might disclose the book's fate. I googled the title, stalking the book's reception and finding mostly nothing.

It was as close as I've ever come to an addiction. Even today, I succumb to the urge to find my books online; I feel the basest part of me craving easy kudos, my false self seeking false assurance, and suddenly the vacuous ethernet has sucked a precious hour of my time. I'm in recovery, and I stumble. Effort can bring results, but now I know there's a difference between agency that works in concert with surrender and agency reliant solely on its own volition. While the idea would have horrified me at the time, in hindsight I recognize I was trying to control the outcome. This was my third misstep. When the outcome was not what I'd hoped, I grew desperate, obsessive, and even more controlling.

The Crash

Writing fiction took me into terrain daunting for an inveterate memoirist: My characters' experiences, ethnicities, homes, jobs, faiths, and financial circumstances were vastly different from my own. I was concerned that through some oversight or bias I'd represent them inaccurately or disrespectfully. So I did extensive research, interviewing anyone I could find who inhabited the world I was depicting. Once I had a working draft, I ran it past a range of readers and incorporated their feedback. I did not want to commit the writer's sin of stereotyping. Part of my intent was to dismantle misunderstandings and injustices around women's bodies; I wanted to heal, not aggravate, social ills.

Truth be told, my motivations were not purely altruistic. Yes, I subscribed to the literary version of the Hippocratic oath—do no harm. But I also harbored within me (and still do) the need to be *seen* as justice-seeking. I was thorough in my research because I didn't want others, especially my colleagues and students, to think ill of me.

Shortly after the book came out, I received an email from a colleague I respect saying she'd found my depiction of one dimension of my main character's identity to be not just false but manipulative. I'd used an important aspect of her experience as a shallow maneuver in my plot, thereby perpetuating stereotypes. She accused me of not doing my research; she asked why I hadn't sought her feedback during the book's development.

That this attribute was something I might misrepresent had never crossed my mind. I was devastated. I felt ashamed. I beat myself up. I descended into depression. I hated that I'd made this mistake, that I'd done the very thing I most didn't want to do, and that it had negative ramifications on a reader and on our relationship. I had failed.

Slowly, with time, belated research, and therapy, I climbed out of my funk. The confrontation gave me visceral knowledge of what for years I had suspected: Writers will *always* make mistakes, and these mistakes will be very public. They might even—dare I say they will likely?—hurt others. This is simply what happens.

I am exceedingly flawed as a writer. Some of my flaws are aesthetic, some are moral, some are grammatical. Some cause minor irritations for the reader; others cause harm. Up until my colleague called me on my oversight, I believed my job was to do my darnedest, and that good will and intentions would erase my error. Now I know that even though I do my darnedest, errors are inevitable.

In the end, I'm grateful to my colleague. She unseated my overactive ego. She caused me to crash. She forced me to look directly at and claim my human limitations. Much of what I've learned about putting a book into the world springs from this humiliation.

The Gifts of Wrong Turns

Time passed. I quit marketing the book, immersed myself in writing *Living Revision*, and began a serious contemplative practice, which has proven helpful at tempering the obstructions of my ego. Striving for perfection and success had been disastrous, so what if I aimed for wholeness, love, justice, and integrity instead? These encompass human frailty; they embrace rather than eliminate brokenness. If a writer orients her heart in these directions, what are the consequences?

The ultimately flawed nature of my work, I decided, isn't the final word. Of course I should try my best—to be kind, respectful, artful, thoughtful. The fact that I'll fail needn't stop me because the process itself is valuable and the product can also be valuable, and what else are we meant to do? We are broken people, but we're not defined by our brokenness. My book is flawed and still worthy of existing. This is the work of compassion. Once we accept our limitations, we're liberated from the constant strain of avoiding or eradicating them.

On the other side of the novel's stressful launch was an unexpected, healthier relationship to humility. When we feel humiliated, we identify with our shame. It's miserable. Practicing humility, on the other hand, is the act of accepting shortcomings and striving to overcome them, all the while disallowing their power to define us. I make mistakes and can also learn from them. Sometimes I need to make mistakes to grow. But I am not my mistakes.

When humility isn't something to avoid at all costs—when it's received as inevitable and even welcomed—we experience a new freedom. Today I'm confident that, were I to work on a book for a decade and not find a publisher I respected to print it, I would either shelve it (I'm no longer in any hurry to "prove myself," and it's possible that with time I might see what the rejectors saw) or I'd self-publish, which I now know can be an honorable (and at times more lucrative) option. There are worse things than giving ten years and all my heart to a book that never sees the light of day, and one of them is betraying my integrity. What my students might think of me could be distressing; they might choose another teacher, I'd lose money, my "literary record" might be marred—and none of these determines my worth or my work's value. If that's the case, my efforts needn't be dictated by the striving of a hungry ego or a market economy. I ought to write whatever I feel most moved to write, and do with it whatever I feel moved to do.

Here's another way to describe where I've landed. When we first begin writing, we serve the spirit of exploration and discovery. As we move into revision, we serve the work's burgeoning essence. But when the project is as complete as we can make it and ready to send into the world, metaphorically or literally, it's no longer healthy or fruitful for us to serve it. That's serving a static object, and we're susceptible to latching our selfhood onto any product we've made. The project itself needs to be in service of something which includes it but is bigger than it. What is coming alive in, through, and beyond the writing? How might the *work* continue to be a verb and not harden into a noun?

So I practice letting go of my need for affirmation. My projects may fail. And I give the release my effort regardless, knowing that what matters in the end is a bigger Story of which my heart and my endeavor are two small parts. This Story unspools with my life and our social evolution and the earth's turning, a creation story spanning time and space toward which we all contribute. Releasing the self, releasing the audience, releasing the product, I serve this Story.

4 Flourishing in Creation's Gift Economy

A few years ago, I submitted an essay to an anthology of queer Minnesotan writing. I called it "Wearing Bi-Focals" because it explored bisexuality not just as a sexual identity but also as a lens for all my experiences, much as my progressive lenses help my eyes integrate what's near with what's far. I lifted up LGBTQA people's ability to embrace paradox as a spiritual gift and challenged our community to grow in this capacity. I sent the essay to the editor and promptly forgot about it.

Six months later he called me. He liked the piece and recommended that it be accepted. In the meantime, he wondered whether he might quote from it. His Baptist congregation was soliciting themes to guide worship during the next year, and he wanted to suggest the idea of nonduality. Could he use my words as an illustration?

I was struck by how my sentences acted like flint and steel, igniting a small spark in the editor. They *worked*, both in the sense of being artful and in the practical sense of accomplishing something—the work of moving a reader. I hope they continued to function at his worship committee meeting. Perhaps they undergirded a year of worshipful exploration, the spark passing subtly and silently through the congregation. Or perhaps not. Likely I'll never know.

I wrote those sentences, but I didn't generate that spark. I created the conditions that made the spark possible. That spark— the essay's essence, or gift—came to me as an inspiration, rising from scraps of ideas and streams of conversation I've picked up from the hidden archetypal roots of the human psyche and from my cultural milieu and my interests. The gift arrived as desire spurring me to write and as the talent and energy I brought to the task. I allowed myself to be changed by this gift and showed my gratitude with labor. Finally I passed it along. Now the essay has its own life, its own agency. If in some small way my bifocal piece helps readers see with nondual lenses, the gift continues moving as they bring this perspective to bear on their interactions.

More subtle (and arguably more powerful) than the agency of the essay itself are the ways writing it made me more aware of my own dualistic, us-versus-them thinking. Now my glasses remind me that there are always multiple ways of seeing. Whenever I actively hold paradox in my interactions with others, striving to see from multiple angles, the essay's pilot light reignites. The living quality of my writing has a counterpart within me that continues to burn.

In art-making, the original gift isn't talent so much as impetus, an innovative drive and genius temporarily visited upon the artist. We call this "inspiration," meaning literally *breathed upon*, figuratively *put spirit into the body*. At times inspiration arrives with a great idea, a light bulb going off in the brain, but we know inspiration more intimately as the inexplicable, nonsensical longing to write, as the uniqueness of our voice and perspective, as the shift from belabored drafting into a flow of composition, as otherwise unimaginable cogence welling up from the page, as the unexpected arrival of tears or gasps of surprise. Authors can't know from whence springs this "big magic," as Elizabeth Gilbert calls it in her book of that title. We can court it, accept it, dance with it, strengthen it, and send it along. But we never *make* it happen.

Without gift there is no creating, no creation, no art. Just as our lives depend on each miraculous intake of breath, anything we make requires an infusion from beyond to become vital. The nature of this "beyond" is a mystery. Is it ancestors? Our collective psyche? The unconscious? Nature's evolutionary thrust? Divinity? When makers are solely and completely responsible for what we make, we replicate what's come before, fabricating inside the constricted spheres of ego and marketplace. Newness emerges only with a maker's humble receptivity.

Inspiration is epicenter of creativity. Sometimes the spark ignited in the author and infused in the text catches fire in a reader. This too is sheer gift.

How do we tend this gift? How can we help it grow? I've come to believe that the secret to a lively creative practice, especially after the writing is done, is learning to flourish in creation's circulation of gifts. This does not mean giving work away. It means accepting, honoring, tending, and moving the gifts we're given, material and immaterial, during and after writing, even if we choose to enter the marketplace, even if we don't. It means balancing market and gift economies such that the market supports the artist without destroying the gift, and the artist trusts the gift rather than income or popularity or recognition as the locus of the art's value. It means remaining faithful to that spark of inspiration, come what may.

We already know how capitalism works, what it rewards, and the culture that has formed as a consequence. Writers are bombarded with resources on publishing, developing a platform, marketing, and ten easy steps to becoming a best seller. Capitalism so dominates contemporary writers' psyches, we've forgotten that sharing our work can and likely should be more than a market transaction. During this end stage, we're rarely told how to nurture our love of writing, how to treat inspiration with respect, or how to tend our well-being. These dwell in the hidden stream of the gift economy, which flows under, in, and beyond the market.

To properly steward the gifts we've received, most of us need to shake up our conditioning around gifts, products, and commerce. We need to dive into the subtle waters of gift circulation to learn how gifts ripple outward.

All of us have dipped our toes in gift economies—the natural and cultural ways gifts course through our lives. Parents know a gift economy in the interdependent networks that exchange childcare or carpools or hand-me-downs. Houses of worship pass around the offering plate, deliver meals to the home-bound, lay out funeral spreads of cold cut sandwiches and potato salad, or, in my case, clothe me after I lost everything in a fire; friendships are sustained and communities served in an open circle of giving. Neighbors foster the gift economy when we share news or lawn mowers or advice, or, like Kurt across the alley, snow-blow an entire block's sidewalks. All volunteers offer their time and energy in a vast network of exchange. Poor and working-class communities are adept at sharing resources, as are disabled communities. Long-standing traditions of circulating gifts for the benefit of the whole undergird Indigenous ethics and relationships. Community radio, public libraries, potluck dinners, Wikipedia, citizen scientists, the Buy Nothing Project, couch-surfing, home sharing, blood banks, Burning Man—gift economies are scattered throughout and integrated into our days. When my father's kidneys failed, he participated in the global gift economy of organ transplants; a kind stranger in another city had signed an organ donation card, transforming the untimely car accident that killed her into an invaluable gift for my family. My sister and I have signed organ donation cards in hopes that we might do the same for others. "Pay it forward," we say.

Wherever interdependent relationships thrive, gifts circulate. The natural world is our first and best model, offering water, air, soil, and sun in abundance, wantonly making death into life, species feeding upon and feeding others in a vastly balanced system.   According to Sami professor Rauna Kuokkanen, traditional worldviews that honor reciprocity and responsible community participation generally perceive "the natural environment as a living entity which gives its gifts and abundance to people if it is treated with respect and gratitude" (from her essay, "The Gift Logic of Indigenous Philosophies"). Buffalo give their lives in exchange for reverence. Spring water gives itself to thirsty humans in exchange for care. At our core, we know the interdependent web of which we are a small part.

Likewise with parental love; what nurture we receive in childhood contributes to an intergenerational pattern of wellness and generosity. Scholar Genevieve Vaughan posits in *The Maternal Roots of the Gift Economy* that motherhood was the original human gift economy; matriarchal societies translated maternity into a social principle, distributing goods and services according to people's needs. Gift economies are broad streams of munificence and humble receptivity; they function on a plane and timeframe of a different order from the material this-for-that competition and dominance of capitalism.

Because gift economies are not formalized systems so much as strands of relationships interlaced over time, they usually coexist with transactional exchanges of money and goods. Most traditional small-scale cultures with ritualized gift economies also operate within a market economy—just as writers do. Unlike money and goods, gifts transition easily between material, relational, and spiritual realms. The hot dish delivered to a grieving friend nourishes body, fuels an appreciation for compassion, generates gratitude, and resurfaces in the receiver's generosity. It feeds an untraceable circle of kindness. A nudge to name a secret in a journal morphs into a memoir that heals its author's trauma and leaps into a reader's impulse to finally seek professional help. Gifts are slippery and subtle.

The currency of gift economies is social, oriented toward the formation of relationships. Yvette Abrahams, writing about Indigenous South Africans in a chapter of Vaughan's book, says, "When you give me a gift, it's saying you want to be part of me. Me giving you a gift is saying, 'Yes, I like you. Let's be in a community together.'" Gifts are symbols of relatedness. "Fundamentally we give because we are given to, and the biggest thing that we were given, of course, is creation. . . . When I give, I am giving from the divine in me to the divine in you. We are one creator, one world. The two of us, as aspects of the creator, are sharing in a joint creation." By binding humans to one another, gifts also connect us to the ultimate giver—our source. Our capacity for relationship includes every dimension of creation.

Robin Wall Kimmerer, essayist, environmental biologist, and enrolled member of the Citizen Potawatomi Nation, offers a model in her essay, "The Serviceberry: An Economy of Abundance." While the native serviceberry competes with surrounding trees for light, water, and nitrogen, it also lifts up fruit to the birds, who then digest and scatter the seeds. "Security is ensured by nurturing the bonds of reciprocity," she observes. Referencing the story of an anthropologist puzzled by why a successful hunter held a feast for his village rather than preserving the meat for the long winter, Kimmerer says, "You can store your meat in your own pantry or in the belly of your brother. Both have the result of keeping hunger at bay but with very different consequences."

I share Kimmerer's story to highlight the gift's power: True wealth and security come not from an illusion of self-sufficiency but from the quality of our relationships. Yes, Kimmerer continues, the farmer who shares her serviceberries with the neighbors despite the profit loss, and even the serviceberry itself putting energy into fruit for the birds, "have to pay the bills and are part of the market economy. But with every commodity traded, they add something that cannot be commodified and is therefore even more valuable." This added quality—gratitude, respect, meaningful connection, love—is what makes of berries a gift. "To name the world as gift is to feel one's membership in the web of reciprocity," Kimmerer writes. "It makes you happy, and it makes you accountable."

Note that we're traversing sacred ground here. Gift economies are invisible patterns of right relationship (with the earth, in our communities, and inside ourselves) occasionally made evident on the physical plane. If we reduce our thinking about gifts to money and goods, our ability to participate in gift economies is much impoverished. Any "gift" given out of moral obligation, cultural expectations, with strings attached, or as a ploy (think the Trojan horse) is not really a gift. On the other hand, anything given freely and gladly, material or immaterial, is. The premise of gift economies is that life itself is a gift. We breathing ones have already received the ultimate gift and continue to be blessed with each heartbeat. How then do we respond?

For many of us, the answer is instinctive: We create. The upwelling impulse *to make*, to become a creator, is a natural response to having been created—which is why creativity thrives within the gift economy. There we know revelation and delight, we find meaning and purpose, we grow, and finally find fulfillment. While we have no choice but to function in a market economy, we needn't let consumerism and materialism eclipse this other reality. To thrive as creators, we must tend the gift.

5   What Makes a Gift?

When I first read *The Gift: How the Creative Spirit Transforms the World* by cultural critic Lewis Hyde, I was wonderstruck. In the late 1970s, Hyde broke ground by applying the principles of gift practices to art-making, inviting makers to see past our usual product- and results-oriented worldview to the sacred stirring underneath. Hyde's work gave me a practical metaphor for understanding the mystical dimensions of my writing life. Because I recognized gift circulation from my practices of Christian contemplative prayer, Hyde helped me see how creativity and rigorous meditation work according to similar principles. Hyde's book was a tremendous gift.

But when I put the book down, I was mad. Hyde inhabits a heady, philosophical sphere, and while his theory was energizing, his diligent avoidance of its on-the-ground implications, especially where gift and market economies collide, seemed too easy, disrespectful even. Being an artist today is *hard*, especially if you have bills to pay. I wanted practical advice. I wanted a method for nurturing the inner vitality of creativity while recognizing the real limitations writers face in a consumeristic, product-driven society. Thus arose a secondary gift from Hyde's book: my drive to write this one.

Economic realities dictate that artists often *need* the market—to make the art, to put food on the table. So we must learn to integrate gift and market economies, welcoming the benefits of each, steering clear of the hazards, all the while remaining faithful to our creation. We can attune ourselves to the two economies and, as Hyde advises, develop rituals for keeping them apart and bringing them together. The artist who enters the marketplace

> must, on the one hand, be able to disengage from the work and think of it as a commodity. He must be able to reckon its value in terms of current fashions, know what the market will bear, demand fair value, and part with the work when someone pays the price. And he must, on the other hand, be able to forget all that and turn to serve his gifts on their own terms. If he cannot do the former, he cannot hope to sell his art, and if he cannot do the latter, he may have no art to sell, or . . . a commercial art, work that has been created in response to the demands of the market, not in response to the demands of the gift.

Actually, even commercial art includes to varying degrees the subtle movement of gift, and those who write for hire, on assignment, or as their livelihood certainly experience inspiration. While only some writers need to learn savvy and grit in the world of commerce, all writers inhabit creativity's gift economy and can benefit from learning how it functions. The gift—the spark of newness, of life—defines creation. We can write in its service regardless.

But before our gift rubber meets the real road, let's rev our engines one moment longer. Gifts have unexpected attributes and function in nonlinear ways. What makes a gift? I'd like to highlight a few relevant qualities.

Gifts arise out of a spirit of abundance. I say "spirit" because we all know miserly rich people and generous poor people. I remember graduate school as an intense, high-pressure, competitive climate with one remarkable exception: Walking across the university quad one afternoon, I ran into a professor, asked her a question, and was astonished when she turned such utter attention toward me that the sun and grass and academic buildings fell away. Her many responsibilities (and, as I later learned, financial struggles) did not detract from the plentitude of her presence, which she offered freely. She operated in a gift economy of time.

Unlike market economies, which are fueled by scarcity, gift economies arise from abundance. Material abundance, the easiest to recognize because it's tangible and quantifiable, is just one arena among many from which we can give. We might have abundant humor or hope, skill or friendships, heritage or culture, knowledge, faith, kindness, time, or energy. Everyone has the gifts of life, personhood, and experience. We each are resplendent with gifts. Only from this wealth can we truly give to others.

If we strong-arm gifts out of scarcity, they're not gifts. While on the surface this makes the gift economy appear inaccessible to artists (whose efforts are usually un- or under-compensated, whose time is constrained by the day job or kids or any number of interruptions, for whom limitations loom large), in practice this quality helps us identify where gifts easily circulate. We tend to consider generosity a moral imperative (we *should* give) because so often religious teachings have been interpreted this way—think the Christian value of self-sacrifice, the *Bhagavad-Gita's* call not to attach to our work's fruit, and Buddhist teachings around meritless work. In fact, giving only because "it's the right thing to do" lands us in resentment and co-dependence. Giving of ourselves takes on an entirely new meaning when we begin from abundance.

This doesn't mean giving is always easy or blissful. Comforting a sick child at midnight, delivering food to the unhoused, revising a book-length work, releasing an intimate story—these take real sacrifice. Our capacity to give of ourselves is measured by our ability to receive. Gifts don't originate with us, they come through us. Opening to the abundant flow of gift, we're better able to pass it along, regardless of personal cost.

What is your place of plentitude? Only from surplus will your gifts emanate.

Gifts aren't free. In a market economy, we assume gifts are free because they come to us free of charge. But the "essence of the gift is that it creates a set of relationships," according to Robin Wall Kimmerer. "The currency of a gift economy is, at its root, reciprocity. In Western thinking, private land is understood to be a 'bundle of rights,' whereas in a gift economy property has a 'bundle of responsibilities' attached." The neighbor who lends her lawn mower may not want an equivalent loan, she certainly doesn't want your money, but she does expect that you'll respect her machine and express gratitude. The gift's price is right relationship.

Consider writers' relationship with the Muse; if we don't respond to her nudges, they cease. We intuit reciprocity when a work-in-progress nags at the back of our mind, refusing to be ignored. When we feel a fierce need to *do something* with a completed piece, I believe a fraction of this impulse springs from our intuition that we haven't fulfilled our responsibility. The Muse still has expectations of us. *What* we do matters only inasmuch as it honors and moves the gift. When readers are moved by a publication, they circulate the gift by talking about it, sharing it with friends, or writing reviews; sometimes they make art in response; sometimes they feel grateful; sometimes they shift their behavior or thinking. The reciprocity may go back to the author or forward into other relationships, within oneself, with others, with the earth. What the writer offers may be tangible, the printed work, or intangible, a transformed self. Regardless, the "cost" of receiving a gift is to keep it moving.

In this sense, we writers are obliged to release our work. Note: Not publish; release. To see a project through, we need to complete the exchange. If we take in the gift like a deep breath, we must also exhale.

Gifts move. If they stop moving, they cease being gifts. But gifts move differently from objects. If my neighbor lends me her mower, I can pay it forward the next week by watering another neighbor's lawn while he's out of town. While the material gift is easy to perceive, the gift's real movement is invisible— the affection that forms, the gentle reliance on one another we may or may not acknowledge, the burgeoning sense of security on the block. Generosity begets generosity. Gratitude begets gratitude. While my father couldn't thank the donor for the physical gift of his kidney, nor could he donate his own organs, he gave countless hours educating others about transplants and served his community for thirty-nine more years than he otherwise would have. How do you quantify that movement? My friend who's a cellist in the Minnesota orchestra likens this phenomenon to the lasting impact of music. "You do a performance and it's gone," she told me, "but it still exists."

Likewise with writing. Writers often say they write to find out what they think. To use the language of spiritual growth, we write to come into greater consciousness. This sounds more grandiose than it is; consider how journal-writing metabolizes a bad mood or clarifies a sticky conflict with your spouse; consider how revising an essay tunnels you down a thought or memory and back out again, refreshed. When I write a book-length work, the long undertaking ushers me from who I've been toward the person I'm becoming—from idea-generator to author, from mess-maker to artist, from undone to temporarily done, from recipient to giver. The gift traverses the entire creative process.

And continues beyond the completed work. A short story I wrote for a high school assignment preserved a clue to my sexual identity I excavated a decade later. Today, an unpublished, eight-thousand-word essay on my understanding of mercy sits in my computer, reminding me to recognize this oft-maligned quality gracing my days. Art functions as a gift when it's an agent of transformation. Clarity of thought gleaned from writing impacts our speech, our new inventive capacity magnifies our problem-solving, our sense of satisfaction manifests as an infectiously good mood. We recognize this more readily with writing that's shared; our grandparents' hand-written letters and our favorite works of literature are beloved because they move us. This movement is emotional—we're moved to tears or laughter—and substantive: Reading rewires our thinking, widens our experience, rouses our empathy. It changes us.

Gifts are augmented by use. The gifts of wild strawberries, once eaten, become energy, memory, and delight, as Kimmerer so beautifully describes in *Braiding Sweetgrass*. "Gifts are a class of property whose value lies only in their use," Hyde explains. "The increase begins when the gift has passed *through* someone. In gift exchange the increase stays in motion and follows the object, while in commodity exchange it stays behind as profit." Say a poet, out on a dog walk, sees the orange flash of an oriole in an elm. When she pauses to notice, she accepts the moment; it becomes a gift. Later, the gift increases when she drafts that image, when she composes and develops it, when she feels grateful, and when a reader's breath catches in delight. "Either the bearer of the gift or the gift itself grows as a result of its circulation."

"A gift must always be used up, consumed, eaten. The gift is property that perishes," Hyde teaches. The poet "eats up" the poignant moment with her effort and, afterward, with her gratitude. The reader "consumes" the gift not by buying, not by reading, but by "digesting" it, by "being fed." This is so contrary to our market-informed notions! I first learned the difference between a market transaction, a reader buying my book, and a gift exchange after presenting at a university panel discussion. A student asked me to sign her copy of *Swinging on the Garden Gate*. The soft-cover bristled with post-it notes. Pages were dog-eared, the text was striped with fluorescent highlighter, the margins crammed with handwriting, the cover ripped. She later came out lesbian and entered the ministry, in part because of my story. The image of that mutilated copy has ever since been for me a token of faith: Writing matters.

When gifts are consumed, they increase. An idea for a fairy tale unheeded fades away; a fairy tale conceived, developed, and abandoned gathers dust, and a fairy tale published and read without impacting the reader languishes. A fairy tale told to a sleepy child, subtly imprinting itself on the child's imagination and easing the child into dreamland. . . . *This* is a gift consumed and thereby augmented. Gifts are like the Velveteen Rabbit, worn ragged and ever more real with the child's love.

Only once they're given are gifts fully realized. Put more plainly, you have to give something for it to become a gift. In the gift economy, where gifts are magnified by consumption and fully manifested when shared, gifts flow and are transfigured, often in ways we don't recognize. When I hid my novel's heartbeat from my agent, I betrayed the central gift of that story, squandering what it most wanted to become. When our dog-walking, oriole-spotting poet pauses in gratitude, her intention fulfills the gift's nature. By giving thanks, she *realizes* the gift she's been given. This is why I believe all writers should attend to the spark moving within both text and being—those with no interest in sharing their work, those writing for personal circles, and those publishing for the public. If we don't recognize the gift enough to pass it forward, it ceases being a gift.

The gift makes demands. It wants to move; it wants to be gifted. Whether or not this "wanting" comes with consciousness is irrelevant; it's simply the gift's nature. Inspiration wants manifestation. Life wants to grow. Death wants resurrection. Gifts want to be realized.

Every gift is of infinite value. Small or large, temporary or lasting, each gift contains a taste of eternity and so has immeasurable worth. By pausing in gratitude for the flash of bird, for the quiet of composition, and for the poem's wholeness, our poet's fleeting gift places her in humble, loving relationship with . . . what? The natural world? The creative act? Mystery? The source of life? Here is right relationship. Here is joy. The moment passes but its gift continues.

A gift's value doesn't reside in the gift itself but in the transformations wrought on giver and receiver, which are of incalculable worth.

Gifts, once given, create an empty place into which new energy can flow. "To bestow one of our creations is the surest way to invoke the next," Hyde writes. The release clears psychic space within us (and perhaps literal space on our desk) where inspiration can once again stir.

Finally, gifts speak the language of love. When we want to express affection, we give presents. Strawberries and sunshine and rich soil; an energizing idea, a juicy metaphor, the creative impulse, the endurance to revise; a reader whose eyes widen with pleasure at our words; our very breath; even death which lends our lives poignancy—love language is so ubiquitous that we rarely recognize it. But the essence of any true gift is love.

As it turned out, my "Wearing Bi-Focals" essay was published in the Minnesota Historical Society Press's anthology *Queer Voices*. When I participated in the book launch, a number of people shared their appreciation, but beyond that I heard not one peep of response. Because I'm not the editor or publisher, I don't have access to sales figures. Was the spark moving? Were there consequences? I have no idea. This, too, is the gift's nature. The gift "disappears around the corner," as Lewis Hyde says, into mystery. Who knows where that orange flash of oriole wings, recreated in a poem, fluttering in both writer and reader's beings, eventually alights?

Three years later, I opened Shawn Ginwright's book *The Four Pivots: Reimagining Justice, Reimagining Ourselves* to find my essay quoted at a chapter head. The commerce of the gift is truly wondrous. Perhaps the gift isn't a spark so much as a clear stream coursing through the creative process. We tap into it for inspiration, for motivation. We draw from it to cultivate words. It quenches our thirst. Our very being is formed of and animated by its waters, so it in turn nourishes those we touch.

Our text carries it into the minds and hearts of readers. If this is the case, the gift flows deep underground, in the dark, and yet is steady, available, always springing forth. Even after the writing is done.

Here are some exercises to help you uncover your own relationship to gifts and gift circulation:

- Search your memory: What gifts have you given others that proved significant for you or the recipient? List them, then choose one to describe in detail. What intangible, internal elements made it a gift? Next, reflect: Why do you give gifts? When? How? What happens inside you when you give them? What do they symbolize? What happens for the recipient? What do you value about gift-giving?

- List significant gifts you've received over your life, material and immaterial. Choose one to describe in detail. What happens when you receive a gift? What do you value about receiving? What do you struggle with and why?

- Reflect: What do gifts communicate that other expressions of love can't or don't? How are giving and receiving connected and/or disconnected for you?

- How are you spontaneously and joyfully generous? From where does this impulse arise? What difference does this giving make within you, for others, or for the natural world? What relational bonds are strengthened as a consequence?

6   How Does the Gift Move?

That moment when a word, penned by your hand, electrifies your being, is *real*. When you change the sequence of your short story's scenes and sense your internal furniture being rearranged, you really *are* altered. Drawing a long creative project to a close really *does* synthesize some dimension of your being. A fantastic read actually cuts grooves into your personality and peels filmy layers from your sight. Despite a cynical, postmodern worldview that posits adults are fully formed and don't radically change, despite the prevalent inclination to disbelieve what we can't see, writing and reading have the potential to *move* us from one state or stage of being into another. "Though we do not wholly believe it yet," James Baldwin wrote in *Nobody Knows My Name*, "the interior life is a real life, and the intangible dreams of people have a tangible effect on the world." There's an undeniable, vital energy at play in art and art-making. It *exists*.

Writers rely on humanity's capacity to grow (and inclination to regress) to ply our trade. If our characters don't change, or if the characters' lack of change doesn't change the reader, or if we don't change, there is no story. The whole aim of sharing writing is to move (entertain, convince, educate, touch, enlighten) readers. Great literature—the books that influence us as individuals and consequently define our culture—gains stature not through canonization (or lack of it), nor by the author's acclaim (or lack of it), but because these works *move* us, one reader at a time. The value of a piece of writing is determined by its hidden impact on our minds, bodies, and souls and by the communal consequences.

How does an author imbue a story with movement? Or rather, how does the author write in a way that receives and passes along this gift? "No tears in the writer, no tears in the reader," Robert Frost wrote in the preface to an anthology of his work; "No surprise for the writer, no surprise for the reader." Frost describes a metaphysical principle: The act of writing causes the writer to weep and gasp, altering us, however slightly. Our tears and surprises infuse the text, where they become available to others.

A formative moment in my writing career occurred at my first residency, an all-expenses-paid two-week writing retreat for women on the North Shore of Lake Superior. Amazingly, a generous panel of writers I'd never met had invested in my creative work! My first morning, I tromped through the woods out to my writing shack, named after Alice Walker. I opened the door to a writer's dream: A rocker and reading lamp, shelves with Walker's collected works, a six-foot wooden desk facing a spectacular view of the lake, a dictionary and thesaurus, and a gargantuan box of super-soft Kleenex. *Uh-oh*, I thought. The women who'd come before me knew what was demanded of the writer.

We don't draw from the gift's underground stream so much as plunge into its depths. No amount of genius or skill will sufficiently impact the reader without the secret ingredient of the author's vulnerability and consequent transformation. The gift works first in us and gains substance in our story before it becomes available to others.

Movement, aliveness, the gift—these are one and the same. "We are only alive to the degree that we can let ourselves be moved," Hyde teaches. In her book *The Healing Imagination*, Jungian Ann Belford Ulanov agrees: "Aliveness springs from our making something of what we experience and receiving what experience makes of us." Aliveness *is* our willingness to grow. From this dance of receptivity and creativity arises the fullness of our humanity. To *be* is to *become.*

So: Aliveness in our art is synonymous with its movement. Unlike literary skill, aliveness is available to all writers, regardless of experience or talent. Everyone can know creative fulfillment because anyone can come more alive by making art.

Aliveness, it seems to me, is also the aim of creation in the broader sense—evolution, the movement of the universe. I believe we humans can become co-creators with the generative forces of nature; we're meant to participate by *moving*—from child to adult, from unaware to aware, from thought to action, from individual to relationship, from wounded to healer, from inspiration to creation. We're made to be movers. "There is a linkage . . . between the source of our being created and our own creativity," writes theologian Philip Hefner in *The Human Factor.* "To the degree that evolving nature has created us, our own creating is taken up into that nature, so that we are nature's own creators, co-creators with the evolutionary process that has engendered us." Hefner is strongly influenced by Teilhard de Chardin, a paleontologist, geologist, banished priest and mystic, who believed that growth in any one person's consciousness contributes to cosmic evolution. The universe careens toward greater diversity and unity. Private transformation contributes to collective creation.

When we navigate change consciously and coherently, we become agents of conscious evolution – literally, *we are life, change and evolution being conscious of itself.* We are evolutionaries – shaping and being shaped by the growing edge of consciousness. When we bring awareness to the process, we influence outcomes.

—Samantha Sweetwater,
Dancing Freedom

This is a leap of faith few people are willing to make. I certainly have doubts. In the face of climate crisis and systemic racism and threats to our democracy, my own sphere of influence seems minuscule. What possible contribution can a moment at the laptop, weeping as I shape my mother's death into an essay, offer our intractable social ills? Especially if that story never sees the light of day? Yet nonetheless it matters. Through writing, I love my mother back into being. I rise from my writing desk strangely cleansed; over lunch I'm kinder to my partner. My mother now resides (however crudely) on a page; her flesh has become words that accompany me, consciously or not, the memories both contained and energized. I feel expansive. In an age when facts are called into question, I lay down a trustworthy touchstone: I know something true. Writing stirs me, and the stirring satisfies.

Even if I can't fathom my own internal shifts as contributing to the universe's evolution—which on most days I can't—my choice to behave as if this is so, regardless, lifts me from despair toward hope, fruitlessness toward abundance, and restless discontent toward internal peace. So what if I'm delusional? Whatever makes me come more alive—writing in my journal, spending a decade crafting a novel no one reads, or publishing a blogpost that's read by thousands—is worthy of my love.

There is only one real deprivation, I decided this morning, and that is not to be able to give one's gift to those one loves most… The gift turned inward, unable to be given, becomes a heavy burden, even sometimes a kind of poison. It is as though the flow of life were backed up.

—May Sarton,
Journal of a Solitude

The release is that moment when the hidden, insubstantial, creative gift transitions into a relational sphere. Internal movement gains traction through external movement. Hyde believes "the gifts of the inner world must be accepted as gifts in the outer world if they are to retain their vitality" for this very reason. The genuine fruits of our writing are not the pages of print or the bound book; they are the ways we and those around us come more alive for our having written and the ways readers come more alive for having read our work. The gift stays a gift so long as it *moves*. When a completed work quickens our own and/or others' hearts, when it travels from our hearts into hands, speech, relationships, and community, it is released.

While it's impossible to identify all the ways the gift moves in and through writing, here is where I notice it most:

- **Within me as I write.** The "a-has!" The welling gratitude. The aesthetic impulse, an appreciation for beauty. The rush that comes of exploring or playing. The tears. The sense of creative satisfaction.

- **Within those I touch because of the writing process.** I bring a more focused, satiated presence to my relationships when I keep my writing practice. I'm more generous, patient, receptive, and kind. (I remember griping about a lingering foul mood to a college friend who then asked, "Elizabeth, are you writing?" As it happened, no. Funny that she should notice.) When I was a kid growing up in a rational, practical-minded household, the fact that our neighbor built an art studio next to her garage and spent evenings painting made a deep impression on me. She treasured her creativity, modeling for me that such a life was possible. Our priorities speak.

- **Within those I touch because of the content of my writing.** I write to discover what I think and feel and believe. Writing brings me into keener awareness. This consciousness in turn affects my speech and actions, rippling out through my relationships.

- **Within those touched by my work—readers.** Inasmuch as my words bring a person clarity, hope, permission, pleasure, or challenge, the gift moves.

- **Within those touched by my readers.** If my writing has in any way altered a reader and they demonstrate this change in their words and actions, the gift travels outward.

Small as these impacts may seem, they are nonetheless potent seeds. Anytime the transformation wrought by the creative process on you or on your project is conveyed to others, you participate in the release.

- What theme is at the core of your entire body of creative work, writing and otherwise? What unites your creative endeavors? This is a broad glimpse of the gift you offer.

- What would you most like to contribute to the world before you die? How does this desire show up in your writing?

- What or whom have you loved in and through your current project? What invitations to love arise now that it's done? "To love another is a creative act," the scholar Beatrice Breteau writes in God's Ecstasy. You've loved your project into being; the gift resides where love still radiates.

- To help identify the gift within your project, draw a Venn diagram (see next page):

  - Label the first circle with your project's title, the second with your name. Fill in the circles with answers to these questions: As you sit with your completed work, where is the energy, the curiosity, the creativity? What does the project want? What's still coming alive? Consider who you are today as a result of having written this project. Where are your energy, curiosity, and creativity today? What do you desire now? When both you and the project share an answer, place it in the center.

- Try this same exercise using your project and your family, your broader community, your country, and finally "Creation" or "the world" or "evolution." What is coming alive? What might yet come alive?

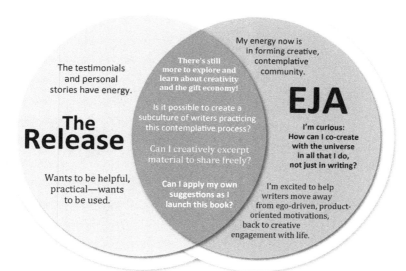

7 What?! The Gift Can Move Without Publishing?

We writers, whose working hours are spent conceding to our curiosity, sleuthing elusive emotions, and constructing imaginative cathedrals—that is, exploring possibilities—have a propensity to foreclose on possibility once the project is done. I'd hazard a guess that you, dear reader, fall into one of three camps: You want to publish your piece, you have no intention of publishing your piece, or you're trying to decide whether or not to publish. The decisions you made while you were writing were born of creative freedom, but now you've arrived at the grocery store of publishing having to "choose" between products. I beg you to heed the genius of Gracie Allen, the wife and comic partner of comedian George Burns: Never place a period where God has placed a comma. Your job now is to support the gift's ongoing movement. Don't presume to know how or where it wants to move. Don't limit the gift's options, in any direction.

For those hell-bent on publishing, know that opening to the interior dimension of the release is key to your well-being and may profoundly affect your publishing outcomes. For those determined to hold your work private, know that the gift often makes demands of us we'd rather not accept. We need to keep our eyes trained on the gift's movement. How do we recognize it?

Let's start with some stories.

When I asked my writing circles whether the life-spark of a creative work continues to burn even when no one reads it, I received some marvelous answers. My favorite came from Erika Alin, a student who wrote a fully formed memoir over the course of a decade. She never published it. The book, she told me, exists "within my deeper being as an implicit reference point and even a subtle source of direction."

> In the years since I completed it, on several occasions when I've found it hard to sustain faith in my writing or other creative endeavors, or in life choices that involve devoting significant time to pursuits that may not bear any visible fruit in the outside world, the unpublished book seems to tug at my memory and remind me of the value of sticking with commitments that have the potential to move me in directions of greater openness and growth. In a way, the presence of the work helps to keep my life on course. . . .
> While the memoir continues to embody a form of resolution and wholeness for me, it somewhat paradoxically also reminds me of how incomplete any final work may end up being, and of the importance of trying to approach all of my writing, creative, and other endeavors with an ongoing sense of exploration and openness. (Whether I actually achieve this is quite a different matter!)

I appreciate Erika's attention to the orienting pull of her project. Writing the manuscript, she shared, "evoked strong emotions; it was one of the most powerful life experiences I've had as an adult." Afterward, she could never un-know that "creative inspiration, even elation." Today it serves as her magnetic pole.

Memoirist Laura Kelly Fanucci told me a similar story about a much smaller piece:

> I wrote an essay years ago on depression during pregnancy that was accepted by a literary journal which folded before it was published. So the piece was fully edited and ready to go but never saw the light of day. I thought about submitting it elsewhere, but ironically life intervened in the childbearing department with suffering much greater than depression (infant loss). So later I decided to just let that piece be. It continues to bear fruit in my life by keeping me compassionate toward issues of mental health and motherhood (and pulls me back to a time beyond this more recent and intense suffering). It was also a good learning experience of being edited as a newer writer, the humility of letting go of your darlings, working with good editors to bring more from a piece than you as the author can envision, etc.

Fanucci benefited from the craft lessons of a fine editor; the skills she gained working on this piece she then brought to bear on subsequent projects. As my mentor Mary Rockcastle quipped, she had to write an unpublishable novel before she could write a publishable one. For many writers, excellence is deeply gratifying and worth pursuing for its own sake. Mastery is a gift. Ideas and voice develop regardless of publishing. Nothing is wasted. But note what's most significant to Fanucci. She tucked the unpublished essay in her being and lives from its wisdom. Compassion is a beautiful consequence of her effort.

Robert Glass, lifelong Buddhist practitioner and memoirist, wrote to me that unpublished work "flows outward into the author's sphere of being." We should never dismiss the subterranean influence of creative work on its writer as solipsistic or small. A transformed presence is always a worthy outcome.

When mixed media artist Rachelle Barmann wanted to represent "all aspects of who I am and who I've been, not rejecting, but learning to love the multifaceted person" she was, she found twenty journal pages from various life stages, from "awkward, anxiety prone teenager, to a mother with young children, to a middle-aged woman facing a divorce."

> It wasn't until I'd started preparing the pieces that I realized the significance of what I wanted to express: to be a healthy, human being means accepting, incorporating and loving *all* of ourselves. There is no room for rejecting aspects of ourselves or our past. Rather than use copies of my journals, I decided to use the actual pages. I discovered this to be freeing and an acknowledgment of the present. The person I once was only exists as she is incorporated into who I am now.

I love Rachelle's series for how it transmutes old work into a new dimension. Writers do this all the time within our own medium, harvesting an image or concept or impetus from a "failed" project to use in the next. In their book *Art and Fear*, David Bayles and Ted Orland go so far as to say, "In essence, art lies embedded in the conceptual leap between pieces, not in the pieces themselves." The gift moves when we push off from what we've done into fresh terrain.

Sometimes we set a project aside only to have it rise from the ashes decades later. Stephen King said of one project he resurrected after thirty years, "It was like my mind was working on it underneath." Likely the reverse was true as well—the unconscious morphing of the story exerted an influence on his life. In a *New York Times* article called "Why Do Writers

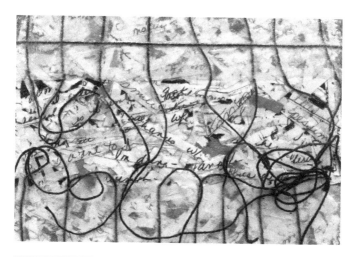

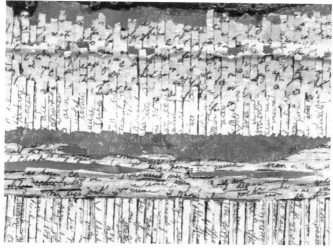

Abandon Novels?" Dan Kois tells how Allan Gurganus spent three years at the beginning of his career crafting a novel that he then gave up on. The story explored a congregation's spiritual growth and sexual misconduct over a century; its scope was too broad for the young writer. "But all these years later," he said, "the dinosaur bones of the church novel show signs of quickening flesh. . . . Now, in my early sixties, I know almost enough." Sometimes unpublished work is reincarnated, consciously or unconsciously, within new work. The culture also changes, becoming more or less conducive to receiving projects and thus shifting an author's relationship to old writing. Creative endeavors have a life force and a timing all their own, which we can learn to serve.

An editor shared this story with me. When her husband was in his twenties, his father, with whom he'd had a troubled relationship, committed suicide. Shortly afterward, he wrote an essay chronicling significant, sweet, formative memories of his father. I can't remember whether or not he published the essay; this detail is irrelevant. A few years later, some skeletons fell out of the family closet that caused the writer to furiously disown his father. He felt betrayed, ashamed, and deeply angry.

Because his wife was afraid he would destroy the essay, she hid a copy. Her husband was right to be angry, she felt, but the essay also contained a truth. It preserves for her husband a fragment of good in his relationship until a time when he can embrace it along with the bad.

Completed writing holds outside of us what we can't always contain in our being. My editor friend recognized a gift in the essay that its author could not. She chose to protect it.

Daniel Wallace, the author of six novels including *Big Fish,* a *New York Times* bestseller, tells in his article "Rejection Slips" how he tried for more than thirty years and with over fifty stories to publish in *The New Yorker.* When he first began submitting in 1984, he thought *The New Yorker* epitomized literary success. His stories landed on the desk of editor Daniel Menaker, who eventually jotted "a little something" on the rejected pages. "I had no idea who this person was," Wallace wrote, "and it didn't really matter because at that time in my life, editors were all-powerful demigods whose approval would allow me entry into the world I hungrily watched from afar." Over six years, Menaker's rejections grew personal—an encouraging sign. One story he even called "very good. . . . as far as it goes." He invited Wallace to continue submitting.

Eventually Menaker left *The New Yorker* to become editor-in-chief at Random House, and then left publishing to teach in an MFA program. For years, *The New Yorker* continued to reject Wallace's submissions despite the commercial success of his books. Then, on a whim, Wallace looked Menaker up. Menaker remembered him and agreed to meet over a meal, which turned out to be ordinary and connective. They've been in touch ever since.

"Do you see what just happened?" Wallace asks us. "After a lifetime of rejection, I had been accepted. I had made a friend."

What I find remarkable about Wallace's account is how he saw potential within a history of rejections. He found a spark of life underneath decades of seeming failures and fueled it into a relationship. His story is also a reminder that gifts are unfathomable; we never know where or when they might appear.

Marty, my student of many years, was born to a conservative Christian family in a virulently narrow-minded community in Wyoming. When Marty announced at church that he was gay, his pastor met with him, attempting to reprogram Marty to be heterosexual. Because Marty was a lawyer and a voracious reader, this involved years of in-depth theological study and long, strained conversations. Marty was also an alcoholic, and one day after coming out of a gay bar he was beaten so severely, he almost died. I met Marty decades later, after he'd sobered up, reconciled with his sexual identity, left his law practice, recovered his faith, and begun a memoir. Being bludgeoned in the head with concrete, he'd realized, was a cakewalk compared with suffering protracted theological abuse from his pastor and community. He wanted to write that story.

Never have I read a recovery memoir that was so rippingly hilarious, emotionally astute, and theologically provocative.

Marty was a fantastic writer. He worked on that tome (three volumes!) for more than ten years. It was one of the most exciting projects I've ever supported.

During that time, he continued talking with his former pastor. Even as Marty came to terms with the hurt this man had inflicted, he recognized the pastor's efforts as expressions of genuine concern. Their relationship developed into a friendship, albeit with extreme differences. Partway through our work together, as his manuscript grew more honest and polished, Marty realized that his story would prove painful to the pastor. Writing had helped Marty clarify his priorities. He decided the friendship was more important than publication.

I was devastated. The world needed this book. I tried to persuade him otherwise, to no avail.

Marty kept writing, regardless. Then he was diagnosed with terminal brain cancer. We met for coffee after he received the news. I was awed by his clarity—he loved writing, he loved his project, and he was going to give a reading. A few months later, a local bookstore hosted the event; dozens of people crammed between the bookshelves and laughed and cried through Marty's stories. The evening celebrated his work as well as his life.

I'm still humbled by Marty's choice to value friendship over publication, especially since I suspect the pastor never knew about Marty's sacrifice. Actually, *sacrifice* is the wrong word; it was a gift, and Marty thrived in the giving. His ability to love had grown expansive—certainly a worthy outcome for his project. It's rare that any consequences of publishing come close to being as rich.

In his article "The Turn," Benjamin Percy recounts that, after two years of work on his first novel, his agent made the rounds of New York publishers, to no avail. The consensus was that he could write, just not a novel. The evening Percy got the final word, he slumped on the couch nursing a whisky and listening to John Coltrane. He couldn't bring himself to tell his wife, who was pregnant with their first child. "I believed that the past two years of work had been a complete waste. I had let her down. I had let my unborn child down. I had let my agent down. I had let myself down. I sucked so bad that no one in the history of sucking sucked worse than I sucked." That night, he went to his computer and deleted the novel.

Fortunately, the next morning he retrieved it from the trash. "The book shattered" in his mind as he reread it; all the broken pieces that didn't congeal as a novel rearranged themselves into independent stories. One eventually "snuck its way" into the new *Best American Short Stories.*

Percy's pivot was like that swift turn in basketball, one foot planted while everything else is in motion. Percy had enough curiosity or stubbornness or resilience to keep the ball moving. "Not selling that novel was one of the best things that ever happened to me. But try telling that to the guy lying on the couch. . . . He'd probably take a swing and call me a Pollyanna. But that's only because he didn't realize he was on the wrong road and needed to turn off it."

"There's always a turn," Percy concludes. The "turn" requires both letting go of expectations and willingness to see alternatives. Whether or not we *believe* there's always a turn, *behaving* as if this is so opens up otherwise inaccessible possibilities.

Janice Lee is a self-described "female writer of color working hybrid forms and across genres," an editor and publisher at an independent press, and the author of five small press books. She tells the story of giving her all to her novel, *Imagine a Death,* in an article titled, "Books Are Not Products, They Are Bridges," which I highly recommend. Her author friends confirmed the book's power, assuring her it would break her out of obscurity and referring her to their agents and editors at big publishing houses and much-respected independent presses. Lee was hopeful.

Then, despite their resounding admiration for its innovation and fine prose, everyone rejected it.

Lee had thought that she didn't need "to be validated by external forces to know that my writing was 'good' or 'important,' or to secure the commendations of 'the industry' in order to feel like a legitimate writer." She had worked hard to extract herself from a competitive mindset, in which book deals, TV appearances, and thousands of Twitter followers would substantiate her work. Nonetheless, the rejections hurt.

Lee is committed to a shamanic healing practice which asks her to "look for those holes I am trying to fill inside of myself." She realized she'd been wounded by the linear idea of success, her sense of inadequacy having been exacerbated by the "model minority" stereotype of Asian Americans. "I was forced to reconcile these competing beliefs in me, that though I believed in the importance of radical alternatives to mainstream publishing, there was still a part of me that longed for a piece of that very shiny symbol of success. . . . Underneath a lifetime of conditioning, a lifetime of living with this deeply held belief that if I didn't achieve the right kind of success, I didn't have legitimacy as a writer. That if I wasn't validated by others, I didn't have legitimacy as a human being." By calling this unconscious belief to light, she identified the hole she was trying to fill in herself, and that the hole was an illusion. "It could never be filled. I had to accept that I was already whole without any of those things, and not *because* of those things. I had to find a belonging in myself that no one else could give me."

In a casual conversation, a friend asked Lee what press she thought would be ideal for *Imagine a Death*. Lee named The Operating System, a house that actively seeks to dismantle the hierarchical structures in publishing. She submitted the novel. It was immediately accepted.

Note the real gift in Lee's discernment process, though. By being vulnerable and putting aside her ego, she realized "I didn't have to replicate the system, that I didn't have to play the game of 'being good enough,' and that as an author, I had the power of disrupting the publishing model, of really placing my radical beliefs and politics in tandem with my actual publishing practice." Her choice to publish with a press that shared her priorities, despite its small scale, moved her more completely into a life of integrity. It helped her recover from the trauma inflicted by society's expectations based on race. "If I want to heal, if I truly seek freedom, it means that I have to free myself from the capitalist system of validation that I have been trained all of my life to participate in." The gift moves within Lee as she proceeds according to her values, and through her conscious choice of an alternative publishing house.

When I was anticipating the launch of *Living Revision*, I wanted to celebrate with a release party but couldn't imagine anything duller than a public reading of a craft text. What, I asked myself, is the spirit of this project? Revision, which most new writers dread, can be an invigorating, life-altering process. To give a live audience a glimpse of revision's power, I decided to put my book aside and instead invite a panel of writers to offer testimonials, much like a revival. Their stories of being revised by revision made the audience hoot with laughter and ditch their presumptions. Because they *showed* what my text *told*, the event honored the spirit of my new book and I sold a ton of copies.

That launch party amazed me. For the first time in my career, I had intentionally passed along a book's central gift without the book itself as an intermediary. The book's life felt palpable, both within and outside of its covers, and suddenly I saw how I could continue to share that life with or without book sales. I could incorporate it into my teaching and coaching; I could give small tastes of revision's potential in the book's marketing text and on social media; I could allow my insights to inform any fresh writing I did about craft. Walking out of the room that evening, my daughter asked me what I'd write next. "All I know," I told her, "is that I'm not going to write about writing." Ha! The gift of *Living Revision* wasn't done with me. It's still percolating in this book.

I have certainty around *Living Revision's* gift because of its simplicity of purpose—the book is nonfiction with a well-defined audience. How an author might share a creative work's lifeforce beyond the work itself is much harder—but still possible—to imagine. Recently I attended an online book launch for Carolyn Holbrook's memoir, *Tell Me Your Names and I Will Testify*. She invited three granddaughters to read passages to us, thus framing her book as both a family story and a public testimony. The gift was palpable, in Carolyn's words and her tactical passing the mantle to the next generation.

I read Annie Dillard's *Living By Fiction* thirty years ago and have been uplifted ever since by her conviction that a finished manuscript, unread and stored in an attic trunk, nonetheless *matters.*

> The most extreme, cheerful, and fantastic view of art to which I ever subscribe is one in which the art object requires no viewer or listener—no audience whatever—in order to do what it does, which is nothing less than to hold up the universe. . . . A complete novel in a trunk in the attic is an order added to the sum of the universe's order. It remakes its share of undoing. It counteracts the decaying of systems, the breakdown of stars and cultures and molecules, the fraying of forms.

The unpublished drafts filed in my closet, the boxes of remaindered books gathering dust in my garage—these are living entities; they vibrate with the gifts I knew during the writing, and to some extent I can trace them as they pulse through my days. I'm reminded of Marie Kondo, a Japanese organizing consultant, tapping the spines of books to wake them up. Her Shinto-influenced belief that objects contain spirits demands that she treat books as energetic presences. An unread manuscript is an energetic presence in the universe. It defies chaos. It bears witness to generativity.

Creation is by its nature a reconfiguration of *what was* into a fresh form. If a writing project births newness—by bringing awareness to a buried emotion, by bolstering a hesitant voice, by converting a thought into prose or an old trope into fresh language—creation happens. Whether by orienting the writer's heart, aiding evolution, or some immeasurable tie between these two, the influence of an unread, completed manuscript is real.

But why? Here's how I've come to see it. Writing is a grand negotiation between matter and energy. When we write, we craft the material plane. Every word, sentence, scene, character, structural choice, and unspooling theme is an external manifestation of a vigorous, interior story. "I want to write," Anne Frank told her diary, "but more than that, I want to bring out all kinds of things that lie buried deep in my heart." We participate in creation—in "reverse incarnation," Canadian novelist Margaret Atwood calls it in *Second Words*; "the flesh becoming word." We make a *thing* that embodies a *spirit*. Spirit, the life-spark both within and beyond us—the gift—animates what we've made. A story is a material object love has entered. When love infuses a project, "the intangible rides the vehicle of something tangible," as Charles Eisenstein says in *Sacred Economics*, and the object becomes sacred.

The release continues this matter/energy dance into relationships.

Traditionally, a publication moves out into the world through commerce; the writer sells it to a publisher, who packages (gives form to) and distributes it to a broker who sells it to readers. This movement is physical. Money is necessary to transfigure a manuscript into bound volume or poem into journal or article into newsprint, and money helps it move. People help too, by recommending or lending it. Networks of relationships keep creative work circulating.

But the real movement happens on the spiritual plane. It begins with the ripple of inspiration, flows through the tears, surprises, and labor of the writer, and courses through others, be they readers or people whose lives the writer touches. If many people are moved, the gift's movement increases exponentially. When a creative work brings more trust, kindness, understanding, and well-being to the culture at large—when it uplifts humanity—it participates in our collective journey toward greater complexity and unity—in our evolution.

The first plane feeds our bodies. The second nourishes that in us which is eternal.

Many people write as a stay against death. Our creations, we think, will endure when we do not. But when we're on our deathbeds, our best (and perhaps only meaningful) legacy will be the loving, life-giving energy we've poured into the universe. Only honest, meaningful, caring relationships (with people, with the natural world, with the divine, with our writing or with its readers) endure. The abiding merit of our creative efforts will be their loving, life-giving agency.

If we are our only audience and the process has helped us live more fully or love more completely, the gift keeps moving. This is sufficient.

My dear friend Michael, who thrived with a brain tumor for four years before he died at age forty-nine, taught me that every sick person can know healing, even as they suffer from illness, even as they die. Healing happens in our innermost being, regardless, and often because of, our bodies. Likewise, every writer can find creative fulfillment—can bring a project to fruition—with or without readers, with or without publication. Creative fulfillment is a spiritual state. That which is infused with spirit lasts.

Thus, any project with a spark of life has true agency and value. If you want to protect and nurture your well-being during the release, respect this spark. Respect its material form as well, but remember—without the gift, the art means nothing.

- Write or draw two self-portraits: Who were you when you began this piece? Who are you now? Consider both your ordinary self and your artistic self. What changed because you wrote this? How do you understand your project's role in the larger unfolding of your life's story?

- Take some time to reflect on how your project's gift has already moved:

  - **Within you as you wrote.** In what ways did the writing of this project change you for the better?

  - **Within those you touch because you've written.** Your writing practice has had an impact on you, and therefore has impacted others through you. Can you point to evidence of this?

- Consider the possibility that few people or even no one might read your work. Imagine your disappointment, shame, frustration, grief, secret relief, and any other emotions that might arise. Then imagine yourself ten years down the road, having moved beyond this loss. What gifts from this project might you still carry with you?

8   A New Understanding of Audience

As we write, we consciously or unconsciously address many audiences. Our audience might be a younger self or future self, ancestors or unborn descendants. We might write in conversation with the authors who came before us or to humanity at large. Our audience may be the creative Source itself. Even when flesh-and-blood readers are our audience, various imagined audiences flit through our awareness. The inner theater is crowded.

We write to communicate. Communication is relational. Any time we participate in an exchange where both parties are receptive to change, as is the case between a writer and the page, communication happens. This is why I believe it's metaphysically impossible for genuine creative work *not* to communicate.

When we conjure up readers in our mind's eye, we imagine people who are separate from us. We have an idea. We write it. A reader reads it. The idea is transmitted.

Obvious, yes? But in practice, writing doesn't work that way. Awareness of an audience during the writing process can galvanize us or cause us to censor, pander, strut, impose false limits, and stall. Thoughts of readers intervene long before literal readers see a single word. Without question we need to take the audience's needs into account; the literary craft is, after all, a two-dimensional form of hospitality. But writers also should reserve the right to address no audience. We should protect our freedom to choose when, how, and why we consider our audience. Exercising this right is key to gaining creative authority. In her book *Beyond the Writer's Workshop,* Carol Bly teaches, "If the soul is thinking *audience, audience, audience*, it cannot at the same time be inquiring of itself, kindly but firmly, 'What are we doing here?'"

Elements of Style, the classic primer by William Strunk and E. B. White, shares a radical metaphysical principle here. "You must sympathize with the reader's plight (most readers are in trouble about half the time) but never seek to know the reader's wants. Your whole duty as a writer is to please and satisfy yourself, and the true writer always plays to an audience of one." The self alone is the doorway into fine writing. Zora Neale Hurston conveys the same idea when her narrator says of Janie in *Their Eyes Were Watching God,* "She didn't read books so she didn't know that she was the world and the heavens boiled down to a drop." Each of us is a portal into the whole, a fractal mirroring the entirety. Any slice of our being repeats the universe in perfect proportion.

The path to the audience isn't across a gap separating writer from reader but rather through a nosedive into profound, generative privacy—into the Self, where we meet the Other. A person is a person through other persons, as the Nguni word *ubuntu* reminds us, or as Archbishop Desmond Tutu defined it in *No Future without Forgiveness,* "My humanity is caught up, is inextricably bound up, in what is yours." I imagine this dynamic as an inverted horseshoe with writer and reader seated at either end. We can see each other; sometimes we can talk to each other. On the surface we appear to be distinct people. We are, and we're not. During the writing process, writers dive through the individual self into our collective humanity and back up again into the particular needs, desires, and interests of another person, the reader.

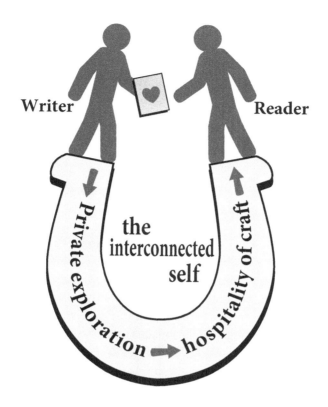

Writer

Reader

Private exploration → hospitality of craft

the interconnected self

This is why, as Brenda Ueland suggests in *If You Want to Write*, "The more you wish to describe a Universal the more minutely and truthfully you must describe a Particular"—a governing principle of literary work. Only by beginning with the specifics of one life can we access that well of collective humanity and then craft our material for another. In her novel *The Heat of the Day*, Elizabeth Bowen describes it this way: "To turn from everything to one face is to find oneself face to face with everything."

When writers fully develop a creative work that is capable of but never reaches an audience, they have nonetheless taken and reaped the benefits of this journey. Crafting a piece is a significant spiritual practice even if we have no intention of sharing because the process ushers us into and across this unitive

When a writer shuts himself up in a room for years on end to hone his craft—to create a world—if he uses his secret wounds as his starting point, he is, whether he knows it or not, putting a great faith in humanity.... All true literature rises from this childish, hopeful certainty that all people resemble each other.

—Orhan Pamuk,
Nobel Prize acceptance speech

landscape. This is the subject of my book, *Living Revision*.

For this reason, I advise writers to cloak themselves in a cloud of privacy during early composition. We can cultivate our interior freedom, postponing thoughts of audience for a later stage of development. Novelist Swati Avasthi told me she imagines this as an inner playground, safely fenced, a refuge she refuses to compromise. Just as relentless awareness of an assumed white American audience can cripple writers of culture, writing to *any* external audience, especially in the early stages of a project, crimps writers' liberty. It damages our capacity to find our truest voice and diminishes our receptivity to the spirit moving through the work. Yes, audience energizes and focuses us; it tempers our content and holds us accountable. *Of course* we should consider our readers—later on, if we plan to share the work. But if we never permit ourselves true solitude, we're cut off from a crucial source of the gift.

I recommend drafting with the door closed, then slowly, thoughtfully, opening the door. Along the timeline of a typical writing process, intentional consideration of readers begins partway:

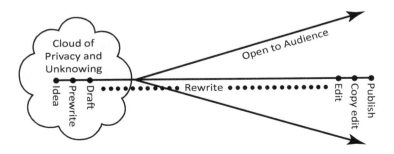

Only in revision do I begin crafting my text for imaginary, curious, supportive readers. Later I bring in literal readers and consider possible cynics or nay-sayers; they challenge me to improve, be accurate, and consider alternative perspectives. Lastly I welcome those with a stake in my project (family, friends), the general public, and readers from worldviews or cultures or identities I might not yet have accommodated. I carry my project journal throughout, retreating to my cloud of privacy well into the release. (You can learn more about this timeline for the writing process in the "So What?" chapter of *Living Revision*.)

All this is to say that we can be deliberate about when, where, how, and why we invite audience into our awareness. We can modulate our relationship over time. Our creative liberty depends on it.

So audience isn't monolithic, nor is it static. Audience is fluid, multidimensional, and changing. It's a consciousness we enter gradually that brings our work depth and breadth. The English noun 'audience' is rooted in the Latin *audire*, to hear. Imagine for a moment the word *audience* functioning as a verb. As writers, we audience inspiration; we are the first audience. The page audiences our innermost being; the page becomes our second audience. We audience the embryonic heartbeat of the draft in the call-and-response of revision. The finished draft audiences the rumbling, subterranean energy of its content. My friend Endel Kallas says that "to audience" is to "receive from Source by truly hearing in the act of sacred listening." Writing is communicating; communicating always implies a receptive and responsive other. Whether this other is alive or dead, real or imagined, divine or human, the central spiritual activities in the writing process are these: giving and receiving, listening and sharing.

If the release is the literary craft executed within a network of relationships, we've been releasing our writing all along. Writing for the "other" (be it the page, the self, or the public), we seek connection; we bridge difference. We draw that part of personhood that resides beyond us a bit closer.

The word *person* comes from the Latin verb *per-sonare*, literally 'sounding through.' In Roman theater, *persona* referred to a mask with a small built-in megaphone. What makes us persons is holiness—the gift—sounding through us into the material world, through our physical bodies into our words and actions, and through our writing into images, narrative, voice, sounds, symbols, forms, language, and audience. Everything contained within the text, including its audience, has sounded through the writer, and thus has its counterpart within the writer. The release is the stage when the audience moves from the imaginal and literary into the literal realm. Intention and practice, which I'll introduce next, are the megaphones that amplify these living gifts.

Yes, the experience of having real people read our work is terrific. In our pursuit of this goal, let's not lose sight of the broader audiences taking shape as we write and our work's bigger potential. The gift will sound through any opening we create, especially if done with intention.

9 Orienting the Heart: Service and Intention

When Black writer Kiese Laymon was twenty-eight, after he unsuccessfully made the rounds with New York presses, a publisher offered him and he accepted $1,000 for his first three books. Together *How to Slowly Kill Yourself and Others in America* and what became *Long Division* sold around 100,000 copies and were met with wide acclaim. Fourteen years later, however, Laymon wanted to revise and reissue the books. When the publisher refused, Laymon paid $50,000 to buy back his rights.

Why would a successful author do such a thing?

When Covid hit, death seemed likely and Laymon was unsettled by the realization his books would outlive him. As he told Scott Neumyer in a *Shondaland* article, he "wanted to get the art back . . . from people who I didn't think have my best interests at heart. So if we died, I wanted this art to go forward with my family and [not to someone who] didn't have any love or trust for me." In *How to Slowly Kill Yourself*, he wanted to take out, add, and revise essays, especially those he could no longer "stand by." He wanted to reissue *Long Division* according to his original vision. He especially wanted to extract himself from an exploitive system.

Interviewing with Tressie McMillan Cottom for *The New York Times*, Laymon observes, "The market . . . encourages us to think that, oh, if a book is published, which really often means some group of white people think that it can get some money for it, that it's done." Laymon fiercely defends the right to remain undone. "One of the worst Americanisms is . . . if you did it, it's good. . . . Especially for . . . cisgender straight men, everything I do got me here, so I shouldn't regret anything I've done. . . . . That's dangerous for an artist. But it's catastrophic for a human." He insists we have a responsibility to revise ourselves and our work, especially when the market tells us not to. As an ever-changing human, he claims the right to keep changing his art.

Isn't this remarkable? Laymon splits wide a common assumption about the release, that a published book is immutable. (By the way, he's not alone: Louise Erdrich has revised her novel *Love Medicine* twice since its initial publication, and Henry James famously republished altered versions of his stories and novels.) Even more tremendous is Laymon's public willingness to steer his actions according to his principles. Rather than rest on his (well-earned) laurels, Laymon chose a path of integrity.

How do we orient our hearts during the release? What do we serve?

Americans sometimes bring a certain cynicism to the notion of service, for good reasons: Those who've been forced to serve others resist it because of historical trauma and a sense of injustice, and those who've been served scorn it out of reluctance to give up power. We harbor a healthy skepticism toward serving institutions (the military, the government, the church) when these organizations prove hypocritical or untrustworthy. Nonetheless, we all serve something, someone, some principle, at times consciously, more often not. What we serve is revealed by our choices—where our energy goes and how we spend our time.

The felt experience of service is familiar to writers even if the name is not. When we generate a draft, we serve the stirrings of curiosity, the call of inspiration, the joy of discovery. We learn to relinquish our own agenda to serve a character's knee-jerk impulse or memory's unanticipated leap. When we revise, we serve the rising vitality of the story, tending those images, scenes, ideas, and prose with zest, cutting those without, "killing our darlings" in favor of clarity or focus. True service, freely offered, is essentially generosity. We give of ourselves in and through our effort.

The principles we serve reveal what we value. The trouble is, precious few of us expend energy and time commensurate with our *chosen* values, in part because we're unaware and in part because doing so is exceedingly hard. I've always believed the early stage of writing ought to be playful and exploratory, and yet for decades, before penning every word I wasted immeasurable time worrying about what my readers would think. When I marketed the hell out of my novel, I assumed I was supporting the book's best interests. My nightstand is stacked with books I *should* read rather than ones I genuinely *want* to read, despite my conviction that bedtime reading should be pleasurable. Too often there's a disconnect between what we assume we're doing with our lives and what actually happens. We rarely recognize it until afterward.

By way of example, I was in the thick of revising a middle grade novel, tracing the characters' motivations and amping

> As long as things stay within the realm of personal experience, meaning is not to be found. It is only when that experience bears fruit, when it connects one to the rest of the world in service, that the sense of purpose finds its birth. For the contemplative, the way of discovering meaning is to discover how to be of service, and the way toward service is through surrender.
>
> —GERALD MAY,
> WILL & SPIRIT

up the tension by thwarting their desires (because conflict is what keeps a reader turning pages, right?) when I read Matthew Salesses' *Craft in the Real World*. Salesses challenged me to consider the cultural assumptions behind literary conflict. "Conflict . . . is not just something you put in fiction to make a story compelling," he writes. "Conflict presents a worldview, along a spectrum from complete agency to a life dictated completely by circumstance." When I added stress to my characters' situations, what meaning did I create? What principle did I serve? At Salesses' recommendation, I then read Yoko Ogawa's novel *The Housekeeper and the Professor*. The Japanese novel was gripping, not because of characters' thwarted desire but because of the humble housekeeper's curiosity about memory loss and the language of mathematics in her friendship with the professor. The engine driving the story wasn't tension; it was love. Suddenly I recognized the white American literary principle I'd been serving: The source of a story's action and a reader's gratification is a character's foiled aspirations. Now that I'm conscious, I can be deliberate, generating a conflict that mirrors values of my choosing.

Every one of us falls short of living according to our principles. This, my friends, is the human condition. But the disconnect—the space between intention and action—may very well be the most significant terrain we ever cross. As Cynthia Bourgeault explains in *Mystical Hope*,

> If we really wish to change the planet, to become a sign of hope in a broken world, all we really need to do (and it is one simple thing, but it is everything) is to narrow the gap between means and ends: between the gospel we profess and the gospel we live out, moment to moment, in the quality of our aliveness. . . . No unified, consistent energy generated by closing the gap between means and ends ever fails to change the world.

Bourgeault, Episcopalian priest and wisdom teacher, isn't just saying we ought to find a means that mirrors our ends. She's saying that our effort to exercise a means consistent with our ends is *itself* powerful and perhaps our most worthy work.

This "unified, consistent energy," as I understand it, is integrity—which is why Kiese Laymon is such a great role model. We writers may not be capable of matching our actions to our ultimate aims but we can orient our hearts in that direction. We can grow incrementally in our awareness of what we're serving, making intentional choices as we become the work's instrument, its representative and advocate. And perhaps this effort *itself* moves the gift.

> When the artist is truly the servant of the work, the work is better than the artist; Shakespeare knew how to listen to his work, and so he often wrote better than he could write; Bach composed more deeply, more truly than he knew; Rembrandt's brush put more of the human spirit on canvas than Rembrandt could comprehend.
>
> —MADELEINE L'ENGLE, *WALKING ON WATER*

I invite you, for just a moment, to step out of the box in which you write for some concrete, external, quantifiable purpose (changing the world, making money, expressing yourself, garnering kudos, conveying an idea, helping or entertaining others) into a broader perspective. Yes, you need clarity about what you want for your project. Yes, you need to take practical steps toward your goals; we'll get to these soon enough. But if your first priority is well-being, your own, others', and the planet's, then your ordinary, ego-driven motivations need to bow to that bigger aspiration.

There's a difference between outcomes we'd like to see and principles we serve. For me, love is worthy of my service, as are truth, justice, equity, healing, beauty, creation, and our collective coming into consciousness. In short, my intention is to serve life. Note how, in Kiese Laymon's story, while his decision to serve integrity involved risk, he didn't forsake his desire to republish his books or stay connected to his readership or earn a profit or even see justice done. The first publisher likely pocketed $400,000 from his books; by buying back the rights, Laymon would receive a more just compensation. Laymon's books have done well since. He's respected. His choice got him good publicity. Within the bounds of his rearranged priorities the outcomes he sought were still attainable. While this isn't always the case, and while we rarely have assurance before we leap, aligning our actions with our principles always benefits our self-respect.

Here are some prompts to help orient your heart during the release:

- Write a love letter to your project. What's the nature of your love? How will you continue cultivating this love? Write your vows.

- Write a project-focused autobiography. How did this project move you from who you were "before" you wrote it to who you are "after"? How does it continue to stir in you now that it's done? Fill in the story between your self-portraits from the exercise on page 65.

- Identify your fuel source. What trustworthy energy (curiosity? play? longing? affection?) drove your writing? How might you tap into that source moving forward?

- Frederick Buechner famously defined "calling" as "the place where your deep gladness and the world's deep hunger meet." What needs or longings outside of yourself (in your family, your community, or the culture at large) are relevant to your project? What difference do you hope you and your project will make? What gifts might it bring to others? Insights?

Companionship? Entertainment? Education? Dig under these hopes to identify the bigger principle you wish the project to serve. How might you serve this principle without others reading your project? Are there ways your presence, actions, relationships, and work might also convey to others your project's gifts?

- Write a prayer or wish for your piece that includes both your desire for it and your overarching longing. For instance, I might write, "I'd really like to get this essay into readers' hands, and I'll try my darnedest, but my fundamental hope and aim is that this essay brings a bit more kindness into the world." Kindness (or well-being, justice, truth, healing, etc.) rather than publishing is how I orient my heart.

- Describe how you would you like to feel after this project's release. Jubilant? Fulfilled? Purposeful? Effective? Proud? Open yourself to receive this quality.

The conscious orientation of your heart, this commitment to a direction, is your intention: the first step of every spiritual practice. "Nothing can be transformed in us unless our attention is transformed from passive to intentional," Cynthia Bourgeault teaches. Without intention, our effort is involuntary, jerked around by unconscious forces. With intention, we willingly and deliberately move in a particular direction. We exercise freedom.

When I practice a Christian form of silent meditation, my intention is to consent to the Spirit's presence and action within me. When I draft, my intention is to explore. When I revise, my intention is to serve the emerging story. When I release a project, I serve the vitality of my creation as it contributes to a bigger Story—the universe careening toward greater complexity and unity. Intention steers me. If during meditation my mind gallops off after some skittering worry, or if as I write I catch myself censoring for fear of readers' reactions or hammering some agenda into my draft or hankering after sales figures, I return to my intention. Intention keeps me on course.

Explore your intention for the release. Temporarily set aside your many dreams for your work and its audience to consider what you serve and how you might orient your heart. Write this intention in one complete sentence.

> What we are, and what we have to understand we are, is that we are creators. We cannot escape that. We come from the great Creator Spirit or force, Father-Mother, therefore we are creators. We must own this, and be responsible. We must figure out how to be responsible, intentional creators. That means we must develop a conscious culture, because what we have now is unconscious culture, unconscious practices. Culture is everything that we do, everything that we cultivate through our every day practices. But it must be an intentional, conscious culture. That means that every step we take, everything we do, has to be done with the consciousness of this totality, this wholeness, this oneness in diversity, consciousness of who we really want to be, and how we want the world to be.
>
> —Marta Benavides,
> "Reflecting on Giving and the
> Gift Economy in El Salvador"

10   Establishing a Practice

In the years since my publishing meltdown, I've experimented enough to declare with confidence that a sustainable, nourishing, formative creative process *can* continue after the writing is done. We need clear intentions and we need a practice.

Writers know practice. We "put the butt in the chair" and "write a shitty first draft"—that is, we show up, make ourselves available, and labor in service of what appears. We learn to see old work with new eyes, receive feedback from others, discern a fresh direction, and exercise the rigors of craft. We remain faithful, incorporating each sparkling "a-ha!" along the way. Our practice is comprised of the habits by which we love our work into being.

But after we're done, what's our practice? What are the habits of mind, body, and soul, and what are the practical tasks, that support the project's final flowering? How do we stay creatively involved? How do we enter a healthy, loving,

Martha Graham found her truest satisfaction in the assiduousness of practice, which for her was akin to religious observance. Practice meant "to perform, over and over again in the face of all obstacles, some act of vision, of faith, of desire"... For Graham, practice was "a means of inviting the perfection desired." This type of practice doesn't serve to shape your work into a form that pleases others so that it will get published. This type of practice serves a higher calling, one that has no concerns with whether a work finds acceptance or leads to ostracization because it speaks to a more elevated, even sacred truth.

—Grant Faulkner,
"Rejection's Gift: Divine Dissatisfaction"
in *Poets & Writers Magazine*

give-and-take relationship with a finished work? How do we facilitate the gift's movement?

James Finley, a student of the Trappist monk Thomas Merton, defines spiritual practice as "an intentional effort of offering the least resistance to being overtaken by grace." If the word "grace" makes you squirm, substitute "inspiration" or "creativity" or "the gift." I think of spiritual practice as the intentional care and reciprocity needed to sustain a loving relationship, with the natural consequences of creativity, growth, compassion, intimacy, and widening wholeness. Of course these can continue during the release!

Every spiritual practice involves these basic elements:

- **Intention**—the orientation of your mind, heart, and body; your greater purpose.

- **Service**—a sense of laboring for someone or something other than yourself.

- **Commitment**—dedication.

- **Presence**—the capacity to show up fully, honestly, and openly.

- **Effort**—exertion of energy; agency.

- **Receptivity**—a willingness to be changed.

- **Humility**—the capacity to release oneself from the ego's attachments.

- **Gratitude**—the quality of being thankful.

I think of these as gestures we repeat, like scales on the piano or forms in Tai Chi. There is no destination in a practice, no point at which we ditch these gestures to revel in eternal bliss. We can, however, mature in our practices, and we can apply them to wider and more various arenas. Once we've learned to set aside our pride long enough to spill out a muddled first draft, we can apply this same humility to, for example, initiating a new relationship or undoing our contributions to systems of oppression. When we cut passages that don't serve our story, we learn the pitfalls of clinging, the benefits of letting go, and skills we can transfer to our possessions or emotions.

> I am a cell-sized unit of the human organism, and I have to use my life to leverage a shift in the system by how I am, as much as with the things I do. This means actually being in my life, and it means bringing my values into my daily decision making. Each day should be lived on purpose.
>
> —ADRIENNE MAREE BROWN, *Emergent Strategy*

When writers employ the internal practices we've gleaned from creative work to our very being, we keep the gift moving—we make of writing a spiritual practice. We return to art-making's mystical origins.

Which is why we can use these same gestures during the decisions and tasks of the release. Gift economy, spiritual practice, artistic practice—there's no dimension of our lives which these cannot penetrate. What I've done for myself in the following pages, and what I offer to you, is a reframing of the release as a practice.

Part II:
The Practice

How would things be different if we thought of books
not as products or commodities, but as bridges? If
instead of agonizing about where the limits of the self
begin and end, we moved toward an internal language
for shared humanity and interconnectedness? If instead
of possession and ownership and separation, we moved
towards intimacy, forgiveness, and emancipation?

—Janice Lee,
"Books Are Not Products, They Are Bridges"

I am one with the source insofar as I too act as a source by
making everything I have received flow again.

—Raimon Panikkar,
Christophany

In the pages that follow, I frame the decisions and tasks writers
face after finishing a project as a practice. Here I ask, "How
can my next steps be guided by intention, service, commitment,
presence, effort, receptivity, humility, and gratitude?" Although
my answers are in a rough chronology, they're not consecutive.
Every project unfolds in a unique way and every writer is
different; improvisation is only natural.

The questions I pose are meant to help us focus our attention
and direct our energy. I encourage you not just to think about

them but to free-write in response or make visual art or move across a space or talk them through with a friend. I recommend dialoguing—a fast, imaginary conversation on the page—as an excellent tool for listening to any relevant dynamic presence: the ego, the soul, the project, your readers. Writers write to find out what we think, feel, and believe—that is, to receive and move the gift. This continues to be true during the release.

These exercises are meant to help us stay connected to our creative source as we enter territory that can be unsettling or hazardous. They form a contemplative practice and discernment process—a way to tend that blazing spark of life.

11   Identify Your Longings

At the close of a project, writers often feel a great mash-up of desires—some altruistic, some self-serving. All are good information. Desire is ignition; it spurs us. First listen to your desires openly, honestly, and without judgment.

- Let your fantasies loose! What are your wildest dreams for this project? Be general; be specific; be egotistical; be charitable; be grandiose; be practical. Get them all down.

- What do you want *for yourself* from this project? Why? Answer this question as truthfully as you can from the many dimensions of your being. What does your career-minded self want? Your child self? The self in relationship with your parents or siblings? What does your better self want? Your worst self? Your economical self? Your activist or caregiver self? Your artistic self? Your truest self?

  - What are your knee-jerk reactions to these longings? Name them.

  - Are any of these longings deeper or more honest than others? Why? How do you know?

  - What forces fuel these longings? Encouragement? Great role models? Ambition? Envy? Challenge? Revenge? Growth?

- Trace the origins and evolution of your deepest longings. Have they changed over time? Why? How might this project participate in their unfolding?

Desire is laden with gifts. It pulls us into activities we might not otherwise attempt, like publishing or public speaking. It exposes our core motivations. It connects us to the creative wellspring. When we sink down to the origin of our desire, we always find relationship—our human need to be part of something bigger than us; *to participate* in some way; to contribute goodness, knowledge, or beauty to some larger conversation. This, I believe, is desire's holy dimension.

But unexamined desire is dangerous, and surface desires (for fame or fortune, for example) often obstruct deep desires (to love and be loved, to be whole). Like any feeling, we need to accept desire, unwrap it, and attend to it rather than dash off in a frantic attempt to deny or satisfy it. Desire is one stream in a confluence of information that helps us discern our way.

What would it take to fall in love with our longing rather than with the longing's fulfillment? The Sufis teach that the aim is not to quench our thirst; the aim is to develop the perfect thirst so that we never stop drinking.

> It is the nature of desire not to be satisfied, and most human beings live only for the gratification of it.
>
> —ARISTOTLE,
> *POLITICS*

12 Are You Really Done Writing?

Of course you never know for sure. This ambiguity is good. Remember that awful uncertainty when you first began drafting? And again in the turmoil of revision? "Uncertainty is the essential, inevitable and all-pervasive companion to your desire to make art," David Bayles and Ted Orland write in *Art and Fear*. "And tolerance for uncertainty is the prerequisite to succeeding." Why should that be otherwise now?

The paradox of this stage is that we must trust our sense of completion enough to move forward while simultaneously staying open to how the project might yet grow.

We may release a piece only to have it call us back to the writing desk. With some frequency writers discover that drafting a query letter for a complete project refines their focus and instigates another revision. When a piece is accepted for publication, agents and editors ask for changes, at times significant. Writers of short published pieces frequently rework them into fresh forms for fresh venues. When books are rereleased in new editions (or bought back a la Kiese Laymon), they can be rewritten. "Done" is relative.

One measure of completion is whether the project still has a hold on you. Can you learn more about the literary craft? About your subject matter? The writing process? Yourself? About applying writing's lessons to your life? Ask yourself, "Is this project done *with me*?" If the piece offers you an opportunity to grow, or if it demands more balance or beauty or depth, be willing to serve it.

That said, most projects eventually cease working on us within the privacy of composition. For the give-and-take of creativity to continue, we need a new relationship with the project, usually including other people. The honest answer to the question "Am I done?" may always be *no*, but at some point you are, or the writing is, *done enough*.

13 Wait

Time, distance, and breathing space, endured consciously, bring clarity to our decisions about what to do with finished writing. In most cases, waiting is a boon.

The poet Deborah Keenan once recommended I not submit short pieces for publication until I'd amassed a body of work. I ignored her; I was eager to see my work in print. Submitting pieces sustained my momentum and honored my longing. But decades later I also recognize her wisdom. An opus shows us each piece's place in a broader trajectory. Distance brings perspective; it detaches us from outcomes; it tempers us and our writing; it refines our purpose.

Often the ego's need for gratification fuels our hurry. Have you ever eagerly shared a piece that later proved embarrassing? When we feel the urgency of a piece speaking to a hot topic in current events, we should tread carefully, probing what in that urgency serves us and what serves the project's gift. When time is limited due to age or health, we need to remember that the project's creative juice also flows in us; it can sustain those we love through our words and actions and be passed down invisibly through generations. Do we really want to spend precious energy on the business of publishing? At times financial need presses us to sell work quickly. Can we nonetheless proceed thoughtfully, intentionally, with consideration for long-term consequences?

Time is a great reviser. With some frequency, I rewrite pieces rejected by publishers into something far more

Genuine dedication in working does not seek the applause of one's own time. It devotes itself in dark trust to "a time which lies past the horizon of my time."

—CONSTANCE FITZGERALD AND
EMMANUEL LEVINAS,
"IMPASSE AND THE DARK NIGHT"

effective. One advantage of a long publishing process is its awesome lag time; it can take years to find the right agent or publisher and years again to see the project in print. While all this waiting doesn't help careers or reputations or budgets, the writing itself benefits. As do we, if we practice letting go. Conversely, the hazard of publishing quickly (whether through a penny-pinching traditional publisher, a self-publishing company with no editorial process, or self-publishing online) is the consequent lack of attention to proofing, style, aesthetics, marketing, and publicity. The tempering of a slow process almost always benefits all parties.

Sometimes waiting is a corrective for the external conditions that make the world receptive to our work—think of the memoirists who shelve finished products while they wait for key people to die. Sometimes I finish an essay and forget about it until years later, when I stumble on the perfect call for submissions. Trends in publishing pass. The public's tastes are fickle. Today's backwater topic may be tomorrow's headline. Wait time, whether chosen or circumstantial, can be a blessing.

Or a trap. Often writers delay the release out of deference to what others think, fear of rejection, fear of exposure, resistance to learning a new process, fear of change, or plain old fear. What makes the difference? Intention. Subject your choices to friendly inquiry, looking for ulterior motives. If you are as conscious as possible about what compels you, trust your urgency. When the gears of the publishing industry grind so slowly the disadvantages outweigh the benefits, protest. But if the gift is growing or moving, trust that wait-time is productive. Your job is to pay attention.

- Pause to feel, think, listen, and explore. What emotions are present upon completion? Grief? Fear? Hope? Excitement? Sit with these feelings. Dialogue with them in your journal. What do they say? What are their gifts and challenges? Do they point toward work you need to do next?

- If you find yourself waiting during the release, by choice or through circumstance, ask yourself:

  - What are the invitations of this time? To learn patience? To step into your agency? To reflect? To improve your craft? To research publishing possibilities and processes?

  - What might come more alive through the waiting?

  - What is the nature of your urgency—its blessings and faults?

  - How might you bring intention to this period?

- If the wait is imposed by others, discern its nature. Is the gift moving and growing or not? What is the reason for the delay and your relationship to this reason? How do you feel about being forced to wait?

14 Celebrate

After I finished my first book but before I started seeking a publisher, I slipped into a jewelry store and, as a reward, bought myself the Celtic ring I'd been eyeing. Every time I noticed that glint of silver on my finger, I remembered what I'd brought to fruition.

I see this small ritual not as a gratuitous pat on the back but as a way to mark the end of a significant, eight-year-long endeavor. Finishing a manuscript is a huge, albeit quiet, feat. Most writers are inclined to downplay the moment, postponing celebration for more overt milestones like publication. But this does an injustice both to ourselves and our projects and places undo emphasis on external forces over which we have little control. By marking a project's completion, we honor our time, effort, and achievement. We give thanks for the ways both text and self have changed. Celebrations galvanize us for whatever comes next.

Even small accomplishments are worth honoring. I print my blog posts, adding them to a binder until, over years, the binder has grown gratifyingly fat. Every time I snap open those three rings to save another essay, I do an internal dance.

Here are possible ways to celebrate:

- Give yourself a present.

- Create a solitary or communal ritual.

- Write and offer up a blessing on your project.

- Throw a party.

- Host a reading.

- Print and bind a copy for yourself.

- Rest.

Be sure to celebrate not just the end product but the spirit of the project and the transformations wrought by the process. This enterprise has been central to your life. Can you identify the project's aliveness within you? Give it a graduation ceremony.

15 Grieve

The transition from active writing to release involves loss. That invisible, conceptual realm we've been generating for so long is now whole; we can't reenter without wreaking havoc. Our hopes for the project, which up until now have been anticipatory pleasures, demand definitive next steps. We know how to write this project but not the next. The person we were at the start of this undertaking no longer exists. There are irreparable flaws in the finished piece. We've arrived at an unfamiliar and seemingly inhospitable landscape.

Loss abounds. A person we respect doesn't respond to the work as we'd wished. We submit it to an agent or contest or publisher and receive a rejection. An acceptance letter sends us over the moon, but then we experience the flip-side of elation—grief at leaving the smallness and relative safety of anonymity. We give up on trying to publish a piece. We receive a rotten review. We get a piece into a major publication but hear nothing from readers. The book has a marvelous run and is remaindered.

Loss in the release is a given. The more you've loved, the more there is to lose. When—not if—you feel grief, sit with it. Loss follows a basic spiritual physics, as Nadia Bolz Weber teaches in her memoir, *Pastrix*: "Something has to die for something new to live." When Jesus said, "Blessed are those who mourn, for they will be comforted," he wasn't suggesting we look for a great divine shoulder to cry on; he was describing a natural, dynamic process. Comfort comes when we know loss and experience our consequent feelings.

- "Finishing [a book] means losing something," novelist Charles Yu says in Jessica Berger Gross's article, "I Just Published a Book: Why Am I Depressed?" "I've lost the potential of what the book could be (the imagined ideal has congealed in an actual form, far from the ideal). And I've also lost that period of time with it—those years spent with it alone." What are you losing? Privacy? Control? Dreams? A familiar process? Direction? An illusion? Identify the nuances of your loss.

- Grief contributes to healing. We must agree to and roll with these difficult feelings. Welcome grief. Where does it reside in your body? What happens when you grieve? What emotions and memories come up? Are there past losses that resonate beneath this one?

- What are you attached to that causes you grief? What of your attachments are born of ego and perhaps could be released? What are rooted in love and perhaps could grow and change?

The piece you've created is a *body* of work; it's beautiful, it's worth honoring, and like all bodies, its life will end. What endures instead is its spirit, passing through writer and others into creation.

16 Fear and Fear Not

Fear is a natural response to growth. Benedictine Brother David Steindl-Rast points out in an *On Being* interview that the root of the word *anxiety* means 'narrowness' and 'choking,' which he associates with the birth canal. "We come into life through anxiety. . . . In fact, the worst anxieties and the worst tight spots in our life, often, years later, when you look back at them, reveal themselves as the beginning of . . . a completely new life." To create or be created, we pass through fear.

Consider experiences of intense fear during your writing process. Perhaps you were scared to start; perhaps the mess of your draft or the enormity of the project frightened you; perhaps you were terrified to plunge into the past or address a controversial topic. At first fear stopped you. Once you began writing, the fear was still there; you just refused to let it govern you. Fear in the midst of movement is healthy. It's also known as courage.

When we fear the fear, however—when we refuse to change and fear shuts us down—the life-giving process aborts. Worry is toxic to creativity. The spiritual challenge here is to resist reacting to fear and instead welcome it, attend its messages, be deliberate in our responses, and proceed regardless. "Yes, this is a tight spot," Steindl-Rast says. "But if we go with it . . . it will be a new birth." "Going with it" shows deep trust in life. Fear does not have the last word.

- "Some of my fears laid down and stopped barking once I named them," author Julie Neraas told me. What are you afraid of? Some fears are delusional, some are worthy of respect, and often they're a mash-up of conscious and unconscious forces. Identify them.

- Dialogue with your fears, one at a time. For example, if you're afraid of failure, give failure a voice in your journal. Allow both fear and yourself space to speak. Be a good conversationalist; ask questions; offer your thoughts; listen. Write quickly and without judgment.

- Identify where and how fear dwells in your body. Sit with this sensation. Try exaggerating it. Try softening it.

- "Fear is not a bad place to start a spiritual journey," Kathleen Norris writes in *Dakota*. "If you know what makes you afraid, you can see more clearly that the way out is through the fear." Fear signals direction. This doesn't mean that, if you're terrified your ex-spouse will murder you if you publish your tell-all memoir, you should do it anyhow. It means that your fear needs acceptance and attention. There are many possibilities for consequent actions. How might you be present to your fears? Through conversations with those affected by potential publication? Through changing the manuscript? Through waiting? Be sure to distinguish between attending to a fear and conceding to it.

- Creative movement is never without risk. What risks are you willing to take? What risks are you unwilling to take? What guides these choices?

Cultivate your capacity for tolerating discomfort. Your goal isn't to get rid of unpleasant feelings; your goal is to create and be created. Creation is inherently uncomfortable.

If people enjoy what you've created, terrific. If people ignore what you've created, too bad. If people misunderstand what you've created, don't sweat it. And what if people attack you with savage vitriol, and insult your intelligence, and malign your motives, and drag your good name through the mud?

Just smile sweetly and suggest—as politely as you possibly can—that they go make their own fucking art.

Then stubbornly continue making yours.

—ELIZABETH GILBERT,
BIG MAGIC

17 Give Thanks

A day begun thoughtlessly, habitually, is taken for granted, while a morning greeted with appreciation becomes a blessing. When we *give* thanks, gratitude gives back by enlivening our relationships—to the spinning earth, to time, to the tasks before us.

Gratitude is the gift economy's front door. If we're not grateful, we don't experience what we've received as a gift. If we are, our gratitude simultaneously acknowledges the gift, ingests it, and moves it forward.

For most of my writing career, I fixated on what I didn't have (an innovative style, for instance, or impressive vocabulary or publishing savvy), and strove to acquire these or at least compensate for my inadequacies. Writing was a strain. Only once I focused instead on the gifts I'd received—my talents, yes, but also my inherent curiosity, motivating passions, discipline and faithfulness, the mentors and authors who formed me, my connections with readers, and always, *always* the revelation, healing, and joy of writing—did I relax into creativity's flow. Even my weaknesses come bearing gifts. Even my suffering. Even the injustices done to me. Over decades, the practice of gratitude turns dearth into bounty. The breadth of gifts life offers is far wider than any of us realize.

"Gratitude is our first responsibility," teaches Robin Wall Kimmerer, calling it, along with reciprocity, "the currency of the gift economy." Gratitude both moves the gift and generates the sense of abundance from which gifts emerge. That ineffable, humble, internal bowing when we say thanks opens a path of affection where the gift travels. Whether within ourselves, with another, or toward creation as a whole, relationships deepen.

A renewable and equitable resource, gratitude is available to everyone, always.

But gratitude must be cultivated. If we rely only on impulse or feeling, if we're perfunctory or simply polite, we miss the opportunity to *choose* to be thankful—a freedom often overlooked. Deliberate thanks takes time and effort. We can build our gratitude muscles in the privacy of a daily journal, in prayer, with others, with ritual. Gratitude exercised grows strong.

First turn your gaze on the good work your project has already accomplished.

- Write your project a thank-you note.

- Keep a gratitude journal specifically for and about your project.

- Artists often experience hardship during the creative process. With hindsight, did your struggles bear any fruit? List and lift up gratitude for these gifts.

- Handwrite a rough tag cloud (see page 105) to illustrate your answers to the following questions. The size of your letters can roughly reflect how important you consider each answer.

  - Over the course of writing this project, what has happened to you for which you're thankful? Did you make new friends? Discover authors you admire? Get to know a barista? Reorganize your office? Learn to use a word processor? Heal an old wound? Expand the reach of your imagination? Gain confidence? If others have been touched by this project already, either through your presence or through reading a draft, for what in those encounters are you grateful?

- What have you learned about craft? Your subject matter? The writing practice? The creative process? The literary community? What unexpected gifts were you given—insights, unexpected associations, uncovered truths? What have you discovered about spiritual practice? Your capacity to learn and grow? Yourself—your past, your imagination, your beliefs, your values? What have you learned about your subject matter? Humanity? How the world works? About the publishing industry? In what ways does your life have more joy, texture, direction, meaning?

FUN imaginative play VOICE
great applied INSIGHT got to read
metaphysics lots of kids books
conversations legacy kids
World generation
GAINED FICTION SKILLS
COMMUNITY HOPE

No creative endeavor happens in isolation. Take time to feel and express gratitude to the many people who supported your project. Published authors can publicly thank contributors on their acknowledgments page or at a book launch, but you don't have to withhold thanks until such opportunities arise.

- Which authors inspired you? Make a list. Spell out how each one impacted you or your work. If any are alive, send thank-you notes or review their work as an expression of gratitude.

- List any teachers or writing colleagues who instructed you or participated in your project. Thank them with a note, gift, and/or copy of the manuscript.

- List any "support staff"—family, friends, babysitters, administrators, grantors—and thank them personally.

- Invite those involved in your project to your completion or launch party.

- Honor these people in a private ritual.

When someone gives you a present for which you're grateful, the bond between you strengthens. This new quality in your relationship is a dimension of the gift's movement. Expressing thanks acknowledges and seals the change.

Along with any true creation comes the uncanny sense that "I," the artist, did not make the work. "Not I, not I, but the wind that blows through me," sang D. H. Lawrence in "The Song of a Man Who Has Come Through." Pause to acknowledge your indebtedness to—and ultimate dependence upon—forces greater than yourself.

- How might you express gratitude for the wind blowing through your project? With prayer? Ceremony? By binding the manuscript? By sharing it?

- Gratitude increases our awareness of the gift. When we feel grateful, the gift signals its presence and movement, providing us with critical information about the force of aliveness in our project. What abundance does your gratitude reveal, from which you can give generously?

- Lewis Hyde teaches that gratitude is work; it's the soul's labor, undertaken to seal the transformation wrought by the gift. He also believes that "passing the gift along is the act of gratitude that finishes the labor." Gratitude brings the gift to fruition. How might you ride the current of thanksgiving through whatever decision-making comes next?

Continue giving thanks throughout the release, both to the gift and to those who move the gift—readers you encounter, those who endorse it, those who review it, and those who contact you in response. When possible, express gratitude directly. When this becomes burdensome, practice gratitude in your heart.

18   Trace the Life of Your Audience

Every project's audience evolves. Here's the origin story of *The Release*'s audience.

After *Living Revision*'s launch, I began jotting down questions. Why was the release for *Living Revision* delightful and my novel's a fiasco? Why did *Living Revision* feel more successful even though it sold fewer copies and garnered less attention? What attitudes and practices made one bountiful and another not? Was it possible to launch a project deliberately rather than succumbing to the whims of fate?

At first I explored these questions privately. I was curious; an incomplete thought niggled the back of my brain and I wanted to finish it. I genuinely needed help traversing the publishing world with grace. My first audience was myself.

The more I wrote, however, the more others entered my awareness. Whenever I had coffee with writing friends, I quizzed them about their experiences. Gradually my sense of audience expanded to include a client who had published a beautiful, well-received memoir on limnology and had almost completed a second when memory loss interfered; a friend who had written two stunning novels, both thwarted by a few rejection letters and now languishing in a drawer; students who refused to share their work because they suspected readers would violate the treasured magic of their writing process; clients bitterly disappointed when their self-published memoirs went nowhere. . . . Everywhere I turned I saw writers tripped up and floundering, much as I had been. I began writing for them too.

I searched in author interviews and craft essays for clues on how to sustain our well-being during the release. But I had to dig. Personal accounts are either sob stories or "pull yourself up by your bootstraps" screeds in which perseverance pays off with material success. Publishing texts are mostly variations on making a bestseller in ten easy steps. In flights of fancy I challenged these authors' assumptions, offered alternatives, and occasionally gleaned insights.

Do you see how, long before any readers laid eyes on my book, my sense of audience was a mutable interior construct? Few writers are conscious of this phenomenon, although we all experience it. We imagine that we're addressing certain individuals; we fret about what our family will think; we dialogue with our younger self or a divinity or favorite authors or the next generation. Our head speaks to our heart; the present confers with the past; our imagination converses with reality. The people hovering in our subconscious or flitting through our awareness are everything from false projections of others to the essence we all share. Whether we've been aware or not, whether it has facilitated or hindered us, audience has been present and dynamic from the get-go. Yes, potential readers are living, breathing individuals. But until the release, audience is insubstantial. It is conceptual, amorphous, shifting, and malleable.

While we write, audience matters only inasmuch as it resides within us. Our relationship to this audience determines what and how we write, embedding itself in the text. This phenomenon is inscrutable and significant. We generate an internal construct of audience—we create it, we choose it, we relate to it. This imperceptible dynamic gains traction on the page. Our audience has been materializing all along, defining and refining itself.

You discover your audience at the same time and in the same way that you discover your subject; but it is an added blow.

—FLANNERY O'CONNOR,
MYSTERY AND MANNERS

The release births a substantive audience, but it's not brand new. There is continuity between the receptive listening of our process, the audience resident within our pages, and the real people who will be touched by the project's spark. Our readers aren't strangers; they've been gestating, subtly partaking in our process. We can reach inside the project itself to identify the familiar souls with whom it has been conversing, then look around to find them in the external world.

- List the many audiences you were aware of during your writing process. Consider people living, dead, and unborn; consider authors who have influenced you, mentors and colleagues who participated overtly or internally, members of the literary industry, and actual or imagined readers. Consider the various aspects of yourself—your younger or future self or different parts of your personality. Consider abstractions you may have addressed: divinity, beauty, truth, justice. Consider participants in the cultural conversation to which your project contributes. Then list any audiences you suspect might have been present even if you weren't conscious of them: Ancestors? Your tenth grade English teacher? Reviewers for the *New York Times*?

  - Which of these audiences were unequivocally life-giving?

  - Articulate their gifts and how they helped shape your work. Where in your writing process can you identify their contributions? Where in your text do you see evidence of their fingerprints? How have others been "sounding through" you? How has others' receptivity called forth your creative work?

- Brainstorm how you might continue to engage these audiences during the release. With thanks or conversation? With ritual or prayer? By sharing your writing? With a request for help? With a collaborative project or a cup of coffee?

- Which of these audiences both helped and hindered you? Identify those aspects that were life-giving and explore the above questions.

- Which of these audiences were destructive, insidious, soul-crushing, or paralyzing? Trace their influence on your writing process. Where does evidence of their presence show up in the text? For example, did you censor yourself or perform unnecessarily? Knowing this now, what will you do? Revise? Proceed with caution? How will you choose to relate to these audiences moving forward?

- Who or what does your project address? A current issue, a common cultural struggle, a segment of the population, a moment in a human's development, a particular individual, some question a subset of people ask? Keep in mind that your project has an identity and will separate from yours. To whom does *it* speak?

- Once you have a sense of this audience, create a mind map with you and your manuscript in the center. In the first ring, identify real people you know who embody your audience. Then move out a ring; who are you aware of but don't know, who are also part of this audience? Finally imagine others you're not yet aware of. Where might you find them?

- "Small is good. Small is all." If, as *Emergent Strategy* activist adrienne maree brown believes, *small* changes the world, surely *small* is effective during the release. Even Seth Godin, marketer extraordinaire, suggests that we focus on the smallest viable market. "How few people could find this indispensable and still make it worth doing?" he asks in *This Is Marketing*. I've found this perspective liberating; I don't need to strive beyond my intimate circle. Explore Godin's question. How might your project be "indispensable" to some people? Why? Who are they? Were you to focus only on this limited audience, what might your launch look like? How would you feel about it?

- Finally, create a description of your audience. Ask yourself, "Who are my people? What are their attributes?" Describe them without judgment, naming their external, physical, and social traits as well as their internal beliefs, feelings, and values. What longing, curiosity, passion, hurt, or question—what "problem"— unites them?

Once you've identified your audience, talk with them. Get to know them. Relationship- and community-building are the release's fertile ground. I'm not saying you should strengthen your network so you'll find the right publishing connections or know more people who will buy your product. I mean that the relationships themselves may be your project's next draft—the gift's new configuration. Performance artist Amanda Palmer names this beautifully: "How do we create a world in which people don't think of art just as a *product*, but as a *relationship*?"

19   Cultivate Willingness

During my novel's difficult production, my partner asked me, "What would your main character do?" How would she deal with the mismatch between the publisher's literary and behavioral standards and my own? Emily's question was fun. She reminded me that my book has its own spirit to which I could remain faithful.

Remember how, when you were first drafting, the story or poems or essay took you in unexpected directions? Remember how revision asked you to set aside your plans in favor of the project's demands? Every creative work has its own palpable being. To generate and develop a project, we listen to that essence, consider it, and respond. We exercise our own agency in service of the creative work's incipient life force.

The spiritual practice of the release is essentially the cultivation of a willing heart.

We can do two things with our will: Be will*ful* or will*ing*. According to Gerald May, author of *Will and Spirit*, we're will*ful* when we set ourselves apart "from the fundamental essence of life in an attempt to master, direct, control, or otherwise manipulate existence." Sure signs of my willfulness are when my plan dictates my process, inhibiting flexibility and surprise, or when I'm strongly invested in a certain outcome. My novel debacle was a natural consequence of willfulness run amok.

Willingness, on the other hand, is open-hearted. It's not passive or helpless; we still exert effort, but with intention, in honor of a principle or purpose or life force greater than ourselves. Isak Dinesen teaches willingness in the writing process like this: "Write a little every day, without hope and without despair." This is the middle way. Willingness is the inner posture of service to something beyond us. We bring a full heart to our work while humbly letting go of all that interferes, including, at times, our own agenda. Willingness is a conscious choice to receive as well as give—the relational stance needed to circulate the gift. After my novel's launch, standing in the wreckage of my hopes and ambitions, I was willing to learn from my humiliation. This book is the consequent gift.

We can't *make* our projects move readers or change the world. We can't manufacture the outcome of the release. Just as the gift mysteriously ignited the page, just as it inexplicably blazed through revision, it will continue to burn in unfathomable ways. In Girl Scouts, I learned that a fire needs three elements: air, heat, and fuel. Creative fires likewise need inspiration, the materials of the craft, and a willing creator.

The story's life force resides in you and in your completed manuscript. What does it want now?

- Are there any currents of thought begun in the project that might guide the manuscript's continued movement into others' inner being? What themes ride from beginning to end? How might they flow in your words and actions, or through your manuscript's passage into readers' hands?

- Just as form follows content in the composition of a work, what form of release best fits the content of your project? Are there any hints within the story itself about how it wants to enter the world? Perhaps you've written a "found object" poem by combining miscellaneous images; you could scatter your poem around town for others to find. My memoir *Swinging on the Garden Gate* revisited the Christian tenet that

God infuses creation to reclaim holiness within queer bodies; the pulpit turned out to be an excellent place to share that gift.

- We are only alive to the degree that we allow ourselves to be moved, and our own aliveness reveals something about our art's aliveness. Consider your completed project's presence in your being. How does it animate you? What does it ask of you? As you imagine taking steps forward, either with or without readership, what within you might be called upon to change?

- Consider your completed project's presence in the world. What broader conversations or currents does it participate in? What does it offer? Literary work comes through individuals but rises up within a particular culture and era. How does your project give voice to a communal need or yearning or message? What newness has been born in your project? How might you serve that newness?

- Consider your journey as a writer. What stage are you at—beginner, amateur, emerging, professional? What role does launching this piece play in the trajectory of your writing career?

- Consider your journey as a human in relationship with the universe—your spiritual journey. What stages have you passed through? Innocence, certitude, seeking, striving, doubt, learning, emptying, listening, serving? Where are you now? What invitations does the release extend to your inner life?

- Explore how your writing career might facilitate or hinder your spiritual growth, and vice versa. Might the hindrances prompt internal change?

- Buddhist memoirist Robert Glass said to me, "Some of us need to share our writing even when we don't feel like it." What *don't* you want to do during the release? Why? Is there any larger purpose that could persuade you to change? Likewise, what release activities are you attached to? Is there some larger purpose that might induce you to let these go?

Every choice you make moving forward can be hijacked by the machinations of a hungry ego—yours or that of others invested in your work or who benefit from repressing your work. Practice discernment. According to Marta Benavides in Genevieve Vaughan's *Women and the Gift Economy*, discernment is "about figuring out what we want to manifest as an intentional choice, paying attention, and then creating a process." Whenever you shift from reactivity to intentional willingness, you're on the right path.

I think of creative process as a dialogue. I open my journal in the morning and an unexpected thought spills on the page. I take that thought to my writing desk, ruminate on it, toy with it, and put it aside. A few days later I return, finding mostly shlock but perhaps a glittering image or a catchy turn of phrase. The jolt from these surprises spurs me onward. When I have a complete draft, conversation with my writing group lends me much needed perspective. Call and response, give and take— creativity both galvanizes agency and cultivates willingness.

Likewise during the release. Every submission to a literary journal or agent query is a call, as is sharing a poem with a friend or mailing a holiday letter or offering advice gleaned from your project. Every rejection or acceptance letter is a response, as are reactions from your community or fresh ideas that build on the project or relationships that form because of the project. You then get to choose what to make of these responses. There's no end, no final say, only this grand, ongoing back-and-forth. By fostering the exchange between agency (what you want; what you can do) and the workings of mystery in and through your project, the gift stays in motion.

20 Live into Your Writing's Wisdom

I get tongue-tied whenever readers express their admiration. "Great novels are always a little more intelligent than their authors," Milan Kundera wrote in *The Art of the Novel*, and I feel this keenly: My most effective pieces are wiser than I am. Essays I wrote a decade ago reach conclusions I live into only today. Literary forms have the capacity to hold more meaning, unity, and power than the people who create them. This is why hypocritical jerks can write great literature and why I can write these pages.

Poetry is founded on this phenomenon, according to Wendell Berry in *Standing By Words*:

> The first aim of the propriety of the old poets . . .
> was to make the language true to its subject—to
> see that it told the truth. That is why they invoked
> the Muse. The truth the poet chose as his subject
> was perceived as superior to his powers—and, by
> clear implication, to his occasion and purpose.

Traditionally the poet acknowledged her reliance on the Muse and consequent lack of mastery over the truths her poems contained. Twenty-first century writers, in contrast, rarely distinguish our skill from the "big magic" of inspiration. Consequently we (along with readers) assume our "powers" are greater than is realistic—or, more frequently among women, we discount ourselves as not up to the task. These days it's easy to grow cynical that there's even a "truth" to tell. If we do write something marvelous, we feel oddly fraudulent that our lives don't measure up. Sunk in shame, stymied by insecurity, we lose the blessings of gratitude. We forget that healthy humility embraces both our smallness and our potential.

If our egos don't lay claim to the depth and breadth of completed work, however—if instead we acknowledge the gift moving in and through us—the work itself can point the direction for our growth. In my "Wearing Bifocals" essay, I concluded with the sentence, "Every morning, this bisexual woman dons bifocals and rises to the work of seeing, really seeing, this sparkling, complicated world." My glasses remind me to move away from the either/or constructions so rampant in our culture into a discipline of holding both/and. But I'm terrible at this! Most of the time I forget I'm wearing glasses at all, much less that they symbolize the nondual lens I seek. The core insight of my essay arose from my efforts to make art of thoughts and memories; it signals perceptivity I don't yet embody.

The release is our opportunity to live into the wisdom of our written words.

- What aspects of your project are more intelligent, wise, and loving than you are? List them. What are your emotional responses to these truths? What do your feelings say about your lived values? Do these conflict with your professed values? Are they harmonious? Some of each?

- Brainstorm actions or practices that might help you grow into the insights revealed in your writing. What concrete steps can you take to integrate these into your life? These steps move the gift.

21   Identify Your Goals

Intention orients us. Longing fuels us. Now we need a vision and down-to-earth goals for bringing it about.

First, heed the gift:

- If you don't plan to share your writing, carefully identify a few places to focus your energy. Perhaps you'll keep the gift moving in therapy, in the questions you explore in your journal, or in a relationship. Perhaps your last project will inform your next. Trace and honor the gift's movement.

- If you plan to share your writing, do the previous exercise first. Then imagine the spark of your project igniting others. Write an unsent letter to your imaginary reader spelling out what you hope they'll experience. Write a real query letter. Write the cover copy for your book. Identify at least three different ways the gift might move beyond you.

Next, write a vision statement. Organizations' vision statements describe the world they want to create. I think of vision statements as our intentions made manifest. For example, my vision statement for this book is "*The Release* will liberate writers (myself and others) from external and internal structures of oppression and support life-giving, creative paths of transformation." A vision statement grounds our originating inspiration in the consequent changes we want to see.

- Who would you like to be at the end of this release, as a writer and a human being?

- What work would you like to see your writing do—within you, within others, and in society? How do you envision it accomplishing this work?

- What change will you and/or your writing bring about? Can you create an image of this change?

- What do you want to happen during the release such that you're willing to invest time, energy, money, and love?

My friend Beth Wright, a publishing consultant, told me that the authors happiest with their publishing experiences

> are those who decide on a vision for their book early on and stay essentially true to that vision, although with some flexibility! They welcome collaboration and insights from others, which might affect the book itself and ultimately their vision of the book in the world. That is, the vision is still close to its original conception, but perhaps now with an infusion of realism and an emphasis on celebrating the little successes along the way as well as the overall creative endeavor of publishing.

Vision orients us even as it's subject to change. Your vision also sets the parameters for your actions—the boundaries within which you work toward practical goals. I picture vision delineating a frame; of the hundreds of possible tasks I might take on, which flesh out the image of self, community, and world I so dearly desire?

external and internal structures

The *Release* will liberate writers from

of oppression and support their life-giving

~ Goals ~

- To publish so I can share these ideas.

- Gain mastery over these ideas and apply them to my life and work.

- Grow increasingly aware of the gift entering and moving through my life.

- Find ways to share this practice online and through teaching.

- Be in dialogue with others about spiritual practice and the release.

paths of transformation.

- Draw your own picture frame and inscribe it with your vision. Then revisit the many dreams and longings you've identified thus far. Rewrite them as goals. Which goals solidly belong inside the frame? Which do not? Might you reconsider those that do not such that they do?

- Now draw your goals inside the frame as either images or shapes. Use size to represent your priorities. Which goals overlap? Might any goals be combined or exist inside another?

- How will you know if you've achieved your goals? Arts grantors and business advisors expect quantifiable outcomes; go ahead and write these. But also identify immeasurable outcomes that signal when you've reached your vision. How will you feel? What will you experience or intuit? What shifts will occur in others?

Remember drafting and revising, when you *meant* one thing to happen but submitted instead to the surprising turn, the unexpected revelation, the subject you never wanted to broach? Your vision is trustworthy, your goals are dependable; nonetheless hold both lightly.

22 Play, Stay Creative

A few years ago, I was invited to participate in a panel discussion followed by a workshop at a large, wealthy, suburban church. The panel was emceed by a major Minnesota Public Radio personality; the church flew one panelist in from Michigan. They publicized widely, fed us salmon and wine, and paid us well.

At the Sunday afternoon event, twenty people showed up. Four congregants attended my workshop.

I introduced spiritual memoir and we wrote for a bit before abandoning the formalities to chat. One woman, a quintessential Lutheran church lady, described her writing process. Every Sunday while she curls her hair, she composes a haiku. Then she descends the stairs to her desk to write a check for the offering. She places it in the envelope, seals it, and copies her poem on the outside. "Opening all those envelopes after church is boring," she told us. "I want to make the volunteers' days a little brighter. They love it. They always let me know how much it means to them."

Isn't her practice delightful? She figured out a way to release her work to receptive readers while also serving a need. Her poems become an offering. The envelope is a humble publishing platform, but it's arguably more successful, influential, and sustainable than the church's pricey event.

If the spiritual path travels a figure eight between the journey inward into contemplation and the journey outward into action, the release begins at the intersection, pushing creative work into a relational arena.

Creativity during the release involves others. We form new relationships, invent new means for connecting, bring new levels of vulnerability to old relationships, learn the amplified agency (and challenges) of collaborative work, and discover unity (and complexity) we didn't know was possible in the human community. The central work of the release is bridge-building.

We build bridges with our presence. If we share our writing, scrawling a poem on the sidewalk or posting a blog or printing millions of copies, publishing forms an additional bridge. Regardless, we can extend the boundaries of our interior playground to include the release. The key is staying creative.

I once knew an avid journal-keeper whose deep appreciation for her journals' companionship during a rough spell of her life and stark terror that anyone might read them led her to weld them shut in a beautiful iron box. When our daughter was little and her birth parents were active in our family, Emily and I wrote Gwyn letters every few months. We wanted a record of her babyhood and biological inheritance. While these letters wait in a folder for the right time, I sense them preserving a significant but unconscious part of Gwyn's identity. A few years ago, I dedicated six months to developing an essay I then realized I could never publish without violating a dear one's privacy; today I lean on the essay's central discovery to remember compassion in our relationship. When the bridge is our being, the gift's movement is often secret, subtle, and nonetheless real. The possibilities are limitless—with intention.

Creativity that comes from our most courageous, authentic heart opens us to the Flow, an unseen river of images, insights, and visions where we connect across time with all that has ever lived.

—MONA SUSAN POWER, *COUNCIL OF DOLLS*

Too often, when we want to share the writing itself, we allow publishing practices to monopolize the bridge between writer and reader, both literally and in our psyches. It's hard to envision other ways to connect written work to audiences. But our options are many and ever-increasing. I'm grateful that the surge in self-publishing, especially on the Internet, has complicated writers' otherwise black-and-white choice, publish traditionally or not at all, with many shades of gray. Self-publishing has become affordable, at times more profitable than traditional publishing, and in some circumstances equally respected. Self-publishing is in fact a time-honored tradition; Martin Luther nailed his 95 Theses to the church door, Jane Austen and Marcel Proust paid to have their prose printed, Benjamin Franklin, William Blake, and Walt Whitman produced their own work, and Virginia Woolf and Dave Eggers established their own presses. English professor William Strunk had *The Elements of Style* printed in 1918 to use with his students at Cornell University; the book was only later revised by E. B. White and published by Macmillan and Company. Self-publishing, formerly scorned as "vanity printing," now runs the gamut from glorified photocopy shops to high-end hybrid publishing houses to independent author-entrepreneurs. Writing communities form cooperative or worker-owned presses. Small presses invite their authors onto the production team. And ever-multiplying ways to connect readers with writers appear daily on the internet: blogs, online journals, indie book clubs, writing communities, social media, and platforms like *Medium* for sharing ideas and CaringBridge for those going through illness. The internet democratizes publishing, magnifying its blessings and curses. If you share something, chances are good someone out there will appreciate it.

Given a dose of ingenuity, the possibilities for publishing are infinite. Building a bridge so the gift can move a reader is not the same as building a bridge to sell a product, although they are not mutually exclusive. Consider these examples:

- My friend Christine occasionally reads her latest poem into my voicemail.

- Once, after I gave a reading, a woman approached to hand me a page from her purse. "Now I want to share my work with you," she said. Memoirist Patricia Hampl calls this the economy of stories, a quiet exchange of expression and vulnerability that leaves both parties less lonely.

- Because I love poetry and think Americans don't read enough of it, my partner and I have a little "Poetry House" beside our front sidewalk where I distribute photocopies of my favorites. I enjoy acting as a distributor for others' under-read work. Similarly, a neighbor with a large window overlooking the street posts poetry for passers-by, and the art director at a family camp hangs the "poem of the day" with colorful yarn from a tree.

- The city of St. Paul imprints the work of local poets into newly poured concrete, and the city of Minneapolis hangs poets' work on buses and trains.

- A friend of mine was on a bus in Colombia when a woman distributed copies of her poem to its riders.

It is not enough to know we want freedom. We have to practice it.
—Jasmine Syedullah,
Radical Dharma

- Poets tweet pithy microwork or post their latest on Facebook.

- South Minneapolis writer Diver Van Avery supports an event called "Poetry and Pie," where local bakers donate dozens of pies, neighbors gather on picnic blankets to eat, and poets circulate, giving readings.

- One of the most gratifying stories I've ever written is "Captain Curly," the adventures of a five-year-old ginger-haired pirate. I recorded a dramatic reading for my daughter's fourth Christmas, and it has faithfully put her to sleep for ten years and running. *Winnie the Pooh* famously began this way, as have most children's stories. Perhaps someday I'll polish "Captain Curly" for wider distribution, but for now she's doing good work in one girl's bedroom.

- When a woman died young, her wife put together a chapbook of poems they'd both written, illustrated with their daughter's drawings. She printed, stapled it, and mailed it to the dozens of friends and family who had supported them during the illness. She also left stacks of the chapbook around town, at the coffee house the couple had owned, and at organizations where they were involved. The family's

Self-Publishing

Nonsense I reply to teachers who say no one will read my poems

Ridiculous I retort to editors who say no one will publish my poems

Armed with a stack of my very best

From the library shelves I remove every poetry book

Into the ones most read the ones with the flexible spines

I insert a new page with a poem of my own

Returning each book to its own special nook I count the tomes that published my poems.

—Arona Fay Roshal

creations became an act of gratitude and the community's means of remembering.

- Marketing specialist Dan Blank recounted this story in his blog, "The Creative Shift": After self-publishing several collections, essayist Dawn Downey wanted to explore her attachment to her writing. Painters "pour their emotional/spiritual/psychological stuff into their work. Then they sell it, and never interact with it again. I was curious. What did that feel like?" She was also inspired by an artist who burned his work. "He seemed free. I wanted to be that guy." Downey decided to print one hundred copies of her next book, sell them out of her home, and destroy all other evidence of their existence. "What would it feel like when I no longer own or control this book? When it exists only in the hands of readers?" On deleting yet another file of the manuscript, Downey observed, "Another piece of *Listicles* is released." When asked what she learned in the process, Downey answered, "That creativity creates me."

- A friend of mine, daunted by the long haul of writing a trauma memoir, shares snippets of healing stories on social media. They spark lively conversations and much gratitude.

- A Minnesota Jewish writing lab requires all participants to exhibit their work at an end-of-year show. Their creation must take some physical form that's not just a printed copy. This forces the writers either to add a visual dimension to their writing or to collaborate with visual artists.

- The Future Library Project in Norway is a publishing version of a time capsule. Authors (like Margaret Atwood and Elif Safak) contribute complete but unread manuscripts to a vault built in a forest of a thousand newly planted trees, where they'll be stored for a hundred years. The trees will provide paper to print the books.

- The Brautigan Library, whose mission is to "archive and curate unpublished analogue and digital books by unknown, but aspiring, writers," makes manuscripts available to the reading public.

- Tupelo Press hosts a program called 30/30 in which volunteer poets write thirty poems in thirty days. The press solicits fiscal sponsors for these writers, publishes their poems online, and sends the collection to each poet's supporters.

- Using the Community Supported Agriculture model, Springboard for the Arts in St. Paul sells shares of "Community Supported Art." Buyers are delivered three curated boxes of art, including writing, over the course of the summer.

- Heine Bravie is a Ghanaian Norwegian living in Copenhagen. One night at a gay bar he admitted to a man that he'd been raised conservative Christian; when the stranger asked what he was doing there, Heine replied, "It's a long story." They decided to gather with a few others so Heine could "walk them through the process." Their conversation was so invigorating, the two men soon were leading discussions around the city, all of which helped participants come to understand and celebrate one another's differences. Soon the scale of the initiative grew so large, Heine instead wrote essays to spur small group discussions. For a while Heine and his collaborator, Hacer Tanrikulu, curated an ever-widening collection of writers willing to contribute essays on diversity for the purpose of pop-up small group conversations.

- Writers' collectives, online and in person, provide both support for the writing process and opportunities to share work. Groups ranging from three to hundreds band together to cultivate healthy writing and reading communities. Some examples are The Harlem Writers' Guild, The HerStories Project, Cave Canem, the publishing collective The

Operating System, and RedBud Writers' Guild.

- Now you can find "social story-telling platforms" on the internet—organizations that host spaces for new writers to share their work. These networks foster community, diminish writers' feelings of isolation, and provide accessible, supportive audiences for new work.

- The website *Medium* began as a blog-hosting site and has evolved into a publishing platform with millions of readers. Writers can make their work universally available there or, if they choose, post it behind *Medium's* paywall and receive payment based on readership, time spent reading, and "likes."

- A plethora of crowd-funding sites now make it possible for artists to ask their audiences for support. In a market economy, crowd-funding is an indirect exchange of money and goods. In a gift economy, crowd-funding is a way for artists and audiences to move gifts through a wide circle of trust. Whenever you ask others to sign up for a mailing list or invest in your work, the potential arises to build community. The musician and performance artist Amanda Palmer invites her audience to participate in flash performances, give her suggestions, put her band up for the night, and fund her albums. Community-building *is* her art and it becomes the bridge for her art.

Too often what we call freedom is constrained by the dictates of the market. When we choose between options provided for us (traditional publishing, self-publishing, or don't publish), our choices often are a reaction to external circumstances rather than an expression of freedom. Creative freedom originates within; it is responsive to the world but never beholden to it. When we're creative, we're nimble and relational rather than clinging or possessive. Connectivity, nourishment, creativity, transformation—these are our means and ends.

- Brainstorm a wild and wooly list of at least thirty ways you might move the gift of your project into others' lives. Remember that both you and the "published" work are bridges. Include at least ten possibilities you'd never before imagined. Include some that are silly, extreme, bold, devious, selfless, hilarious, and unexpected. Consider new writing (blogs, articles) that might connect others to the gift. (Note that I say the gift and not the project itself. Keep your sights on moving the gift.)

23 Ask

When my daughter was six and wanted something, she would try any number of techniques—hinting, manipulating, bargaining—but rarely, for some reason, asking. A mantra in our house became, "Ask directly and politely for what you want."

To ask effectively, we first need to be certain about our desire. What do we want? Why do we want it? Can we admit with humility that we need others' help? Can we make our request kindly, with authenticity and confidence? Can we see the humanity of the person we're petitioning? Can we gracefully accept their answer?

We also need to embrace what the Zen Buddhists call beginner's mind, a stance of not-knowing and a willingness to learn.

Reach out to others for help.

- Discuss with other writers their decisions about sharing work. How were they made? What were the consequences?

- Discuss with other writers, family, and friends ways they might support the release of your work.

- Learn about your options. Take classes about the publishing industry and process. Do your research. Hire a coach.

- Seek feedback on your next steps: your internal work, how your personal actions might move the gift, what rituals or celebrations you might host, your lists of agents or publishing houses, your query letter, your pitch, your synopsis, your cover material, your publicity plan, etc.

- If others' expectations motivate you, seek out an accountability buddy or coach or a writing group.

- Find people who believe in your project and are willing to support you. Form a launch team of those who want to spread the word.

- Learn from your favorite authors' public presence. Ask for guidance from authors you know personally.

Neighbors who ask us to feed their cats when they're gone or want advice about their garden or call us in emergencies, whom we can depend on in our times of need, become friends. Intimacy and interdependence never grow with the self-sufficient neighbors, no matter how friendly. Welcoming others into our struggles destroys the interior secrecy upon which our sense of isolation and mind-tricks thrive. During revision we leaned on beta-readers to give us perspective; now relationships are necessary to circulate the gift. If we want to see with more than our own ego's limited vision, others' eyes—and hands and voices—are essential. Asking thrusts us into the web of reciprocity, where we're held.

There's also an energy of love and generativity plentiful in our universe toward which we can turn for support. How might you ask the source of inspiration for help? How might you practice receiving what creation is always offering—warmth, growth, nourishment, change, connection?

24 Exercise Integrity

After agents and publishers put my friend, novelist Mona Susan Power, through the wringer, she landed on the other side with this advice: Never compromise the soul of your story. Never attach your name to work you're not proud of.

In other words, exercise integrity.

When we're writing, we do this by serving the story first, ourselves second, and the audience last—a prioritization I learned from children's author Jane Yolen and have found reliable. These priorities also hold true at the release, but the way we enact them changes dramatically. The labor of writing takes place in private; the release happens in community. Even so, our primary concern is to tend the soul of the story—to nurture the gift, to serve what is life-giving. Our secondary concern is to remain faithful to ourselves by being genuine, acting according to our principles, speaking honestly, heeding the needs of our bodies, and generally attending to what feels right and true.

Only lastly do we consider others. Why? Without purpose and authenticity, any interactions we have will be tainted by unconscious ulterior motives. Giving precedence to story and self, however, does not mean we disregard the audience. It means that our greater direction and self-care establish the scope within which we and our writing enter relationships. Our service to story and self sets the parameters.

By way of example, when I originally described the drama around my novel's publication, I used dialogue and detail to evoke Smith's behavior, thus providing readers with a blow-by-blow, visceral, and arguably more literary account. When I realized this was unwise, I had to weigh multiple, competing values: the impact of a vibrant scene, my desire to warn readers of the perils arising from the imbalance of power in publishing, the danger of perceived defamation, my need to bear witness to what happened, and the central purpose of this book. Smith's part in my publishing experience, difficult as it was, now informs every sentence between these covers. In my revision, could I honor that energy first? Could the conflicting pulls of legality, audience, and ego yield first to the integrity of this book's intent? Could I make these revisions while honoring the truth of my experience? The narrative as it now stands is guided by this discernment.

Novelist Charles Johnson's book *Turning the Wheel* taught me to practice the Buddhist precept of Right Speech on the page, asking myself, "Is it true? Will it cause no harm? Is it necessary?" I suggest that these same questions guide the release. As we choose a course of action, we can run it first through these three gates:

- **Is it true?** Is this gift honest? Is my impulse to share genuine? Are my means sincere? Does my act of sharing serve both my inner knowing and a truth about humanity?

- **Will it cause no harm?** Is the content I want to share, either in relationship or through my writing, respectful? Is my means kind? Will sharing hurt myself, others, or the earth? If harm is inevitable, can I mitigate it somewhat?

- **Is it necessary?** Does the project itself need to be shared? Am I the right person to share it? What needs, rather than wants, might be satisfied in me? Might others need it? Why? Do they themselves express this need?

I'm aware that these last two gates can be perilous; fear of hurting others and a sense of worthlessness stop many writers short. The likelihood of our work causing hurt is fairly high. In a market flooded with text, our own endeavors seem superfluous. In the face of widespread suffering, a fresh voice, artful turn of phrase, provocative narrative, or well-articulated question can appear trivial. How can the water and wood needed to bind two hundred pages measure against the (seemingly unlikely) chance of uplifting one human spirit? We must simultaneously prize our creative agency while owning the real costs of our actions.

Integrity isn't just a personal quality; communities of "integrated" individuals function holistically, conscientiously. Ultimately, staying true to ourselves supports the whole.

A few years ago, I was invited to lead a journal-writing workshop at a large gathering of women activists. As we registered, we were given name tags and asked to identify what we were guardians of: The water? Civil rights? Democracy? Native sovereignty? Looking around the room at the lawyers, political leaders, Indigenous elders, and environmental activists, I felt downright intimidated. I was just a writer; I didn't "guard" anything. A few hours later, though, ushering the group through a writing prompt, I realized my role: I am the guardian of the reflective pause. I protect contemplative time, my own and others'. I bear witness to and help satisfy the human need to listen within.

Like it or not, every writer plays a societal role—that of storyteller, record keeper, entertainer, culture changer, truth teller, mouthpiece, meaning maker, guardian. You are not an isolated individual; you are a person inextricably linked to other people, communities, and institutions. How you spend your time has wider implications. Many people who write hesitate to call themselves writers, presumably because they haven't published. But that's absurd. If you write, you're a writer. A deeper reason for their reluctance may be the assumption that, without publication, they play no public role. Writing itself, with or without readership, functions like a corporate digestive system—a way we humans process experiences. This integrative work sends nutrients to our cells. We are what we

> "This sometimes happens to us, that we write the song that sings our mother across to the other side. That the narrative is beyond even the ethical work we wanted it to be. That it is sometimes a good yarn, that it sometimes brings comfort to others, that it sometimes makes our people proud of us. It doesn't matter in the end; integrity will find its own way."
>
> —CHRIS ABANI,
> "ETHICS AND THE NARRATIVE,"
> FROM WITNESS LITERARY MAGAZINE

eat, and when we feed ourselves creativity, we become a creative, permission-giving presence. Imagine how much more joyful our world would be if every person daily, if only for five minutes, participated in some form of inventive, imaginative, pointless play!

You and I can do our part.

The fact that you write makes you a writer, with obligations to own this role in your wider circles. How can you fill that role with integrity—that is, without violating who you are and without shirking your responsibility? How can you use this position for good rather than as a platform for performance and prominence?

Just as revision lessens the chasm between inspiration and its realization, during the release we can gradually fuse our intentions with our actions. Essentially this is what a spiritual journey is. The more process and product become indistinguishable—the more we dedicate ourselves to the gift's movement—the more effective the transformation wrought by our efforts. Actions that spring from integrity are the world's real movers and shakers.

25 Choose Your Work and Do It

Some mornings on my twenty-minute walk to the office, energy coalesces in the atmosphere surrounding me until, on arriving at my desk, I feel such urgency and drive that I don't even check my email. I receive inspiration and respond with labor.

Other mornings, sleep fogs my brain; my walk is cluttered with mental miscellany. I trudge through my routine—meditation, tea, email. Finally I open my writing file to resume where I left off—and can't find the previous day's groove. I hash out what I'm doing in my project journal. I flounder through false starts until, finally, the gears start grinding. My labor produces the conditions that make me receptive to inspiration.

The same dynamics are at play during the release. We may get a brilliant idea about how to share the project's gift, receive a stroke of publishing luck, or be otherwise blessed. More often, unfortunately, we simply need to buckle down. While at times drudgery, the work of the release holds as much potential for enlivened creativity as writing's other stages. Synergies catch us by surprise. Illuminations abound. The fruits of our labor gradually ripen.

What needs to be done to reach your goals? Do it. Labor is love in action. It's now time to brainstorm which tasks will manifest your vision.

- Given your many goals for moving the gift within your private sphere, which will you work toward? What steps must you take? Where will you begin?

- Given your many goals for sharing your project, which will you work toward? What steps must you take? Where will you begin? Remember that sharing is a gesture of love and service. If you aren't genuinely moved to share, the gift won't move. Where is your energy? Can you reimagine what form of sharing might invigorate you?

- Long lists are daunting. Some tasks weigh us down; others galvanize. Triage your tasks. Which will be most effective? Toward which do you feel magnetism or excitement? Which seem doable? Listen to your body, your physical energy, your abilities. Which tasks are life-enhancing?

- When you resist certain tasks, inquire about the nature of your resistance before acquiescing. Might wrestling with your resistance augment the gift?

- When you gravitate to certain tasks, explore the enticement. Does the task move the gift or does it simply appeal to your pride?

- Which single task might be a good place to start?

Writers generally expect publishers to build bridges for them. Some do, getting our work into readers' hands, but most don't; most simply publish and make the work available for distribution, sometimes widely, sometimes not. Connections with readers are left to fate. I've come to believe that, while writers needn't be solely responsible for building these bridges, it is a critical line in our job description. When the impulse to share has driven and informed a project, we are beholden to it. We serve the gift, and this service isn't complete until the gift moves.

The bridge we build may be quite narrow and the audience small. I think of my poet friend Christine Sikorski, who, while she finds the publishing process excruciating, enjoys reading her poems to others. A writing instructor friend once asked her for a copy and taught the poem

We must pray as if all depends on Divine Action, but labor as if all depended on our own effort.

—Attributed To Ignatius Of Loyola

for years, most recently at a workshop for formerly incarcerated men held at George Floyd Square. She sent Christine a note with a $100 gift card saying her poem had changed many lives and would change at least a thousand more—all without publication. Building bridges needn't require a burdensome effort; in fact, joy signals its rightness. If we can find a heartening means to fulfill tasks we assume are onerous, more often than not these paths will be transformational.

In Benedictine monasticism, monks transition between work alone and work together, prayer alone and prayer together, in healthy balance: *ora et labora*. Work is a counterpoint to spiritual—and artistic—ambition. It grounds us. It keeps us honest and humble. It connects the energy of prayer or creativity back to the material world. Kept in balance, work gratifies.

26 What's Too Much Work? What's Not Enough? When Does It End?

"If I'd known how much work it takes to write a book," countless clients have told me, "I'd never have started."

We've all heard the horror stories about publishing—years of rejections, the double hurdles of agent and publisher, the daunting competition, the flooded market. The challenges of publishing are enough to stop even those unequivocally called to share their writing.

All large-scale publishing (that is, more than reading your poem in a friend's voicemail or distributing photocopies) takes effort. Submitting or pitching a piece to journals can require months, years even. If you self-publish you can hire help but the responsibility for quality control rests on your shoulders. If you want a traditional book publisher, the up-front work of finding an agent or editor is huge—and a gamble. Quality control is *still* your responsibility. Beyond uploading a blog to the internet, most online and in-print publishing demands time and often money. Marketing falls into your lap regardless. None of this guarantees readership. Patience is key.

Significant creative endeavors (like raising a child, for example) always involve pedestrian, distasteful, even humiliating work. Researching journals, agents, or publishers, writing queries and synopses, receiving rejections, tracking submissions, negotiating contracts—these tasks can be grueling. For many writers, the work goes against our introverted, spontaneous, associative, unconventional natures. But so does staying up all night with a vomiting toddler, packing hundreds of school lunches, or teaching a teenager to drive. The slog of publishing, stripped of its emotional turmoil, is simply *work*. "After the ecstasy, the laundry," the Buddhists quip.

Meanwhile, the real labor lurking under such tasks is emotional and spiritual. Do you believe your project has agency in the world? Enough so that you'll take personal risks to support it? When a stranger on the train asks about your writing, is your vision coherent enough to answer effectively? How about rejection—will you let it shut you down or will you persevere? How do you define "success" and "failure"? What's your relationship to power, and how will that impact your interactions with publishing gatekeepers? Can you remember the basic humanity of everyone you encounter through this process? Are you ready to take responsibility for your writing's impact on others? Especially for its shortcomings?

Every item on your to-do list has a corresponding invitation to your heart. If you're inclined not to share your writing because of the effort it entails, be discerning. The excuse of "too much work" can signal avoidance of the internal growth sharing requires. At the same time, remember that for the release to be transformative, the gift—and not necessarily your pages—must move. The gift is an internal spark. Work *is* the practice. The practice *is* work.

Don't unnecessarily burden yourself. One of the benefits of the emotional crash of my novel's publication was that I learned my limits. Do what is yours to do, the work that resides within your capacities and interests. When you find yourself unduly stressed, consider how much of the strain stems from reaching beyond your limits or from your efforts to control outcomes. Remember the source of the gift and your ultimate dependence on that source. The results are not yours to determine.

What is a reasonable next step? It should push you outside of your comfort zone but not too far. Begin with sincerity and with regard for your well-being, then give it your all. Harvest an insight to share with your best friend. Speak a truth that bubbled up from your writing. Do your research, write a kick-ass query, suck it up, and pitch that article or book. Persist despite rejection. Stay faithful to the project's essence as well as your principles. Value the process. Don't pin your worth on the outcomes. All honest work bears fruit, although not necessarily where we expect or want it.

- How can you perform the practical tasks on your list lightly—that is, without attachment to results? How might these ordinary tasks become opportunities to widen your heart?

- Release work often is not generative or innovative. Outreach can be exhausting, especially for introverts. Be practical. What sort of schedule will help you accomplish these tasks? Can you honor your creative needs while also plugging away at the release? If you have limited time, money, or energy, what are your priorities? How can you maximize your resources in their service? Can you give from your abundance?

- Your process during the launch is both the means and the end. Stay faithful. Take care that neither success nor failure derails your practice. If you find yourself overly concerned about outcomes, return your attention to the means. The effort to move the gift is, in itself, valuable. What matters is your repeated exercise of willingness. You can measure the value of your labor by the aliveness within your being.

- If you find your completed piece pulling at your apron strings, you're likely not tending the release enough. Explore the tenacious tug. What does the project want?

Finally, then, we may find our shelter and protection from both burnout and burn-up just by asking ourselves directly, What then do you love? Whom do you love? What makes you feel alive, real, loving, loved? What links knit themselves imaginatively over the gaps? To what, to whom, do you feel summoned? Where does the infinite meet you, where do you know being itself beyond argument? We know again, in the questions and in the answers, that ultimate truth comes from deep inside us and from far outside.

—Ann & Barry Ulanov,
The Healing Imagination

At any number of points after a project is launched, you must decide how much time, energy, and money to continue investing. Do you want to release your project like a prayer and move on? Or do you want to follow your impulse to communicate out the door, into the lives of others? The more outward energy you expend, the more tempting it is to shift from an exploratory, transformative relationship with the work into commercial, self-gratifying, results-oriented ambition. Whenever you find yourself slipping into the latter, stop. Breathe. Return to your intention, and try again.

My measure for concluding the release is similar to my measure for ending revision: Am I still learning and growing? As I nurture the soul of this project, is its counterpart within me still stirring? Does this endeavor feel creative? Does love increase?

- Lewis Hyde writes, "If, when we work, we can look once a day upon the face of mystery, then our labor satisfies. We are lightened when our gifts rise from pools we cannot fathom. Then we know they are not a solitary egotism and they are inexhaustible." After a period of effort, ask yourself where in it you've experienced the "face of mystery" and why.

- As you share your work, how might this mystery pass into creation?

27   Draft and Revise

I know a writer who attended a pitch conference simply to see what it was like. Would pitching invigorate her or make her feel like a crooked used car salesperson? "I knew my book wasn't 'done,'" she wrote, "but this felt like such a good growth opportunity, and a real step towards owning my writing and myself as a writer. I didn't expect to end the conference with an agent in my pocket, but I did expect to learn a great deal, and I did. Each of the three brief sessions with agents was positive—they didn't laugh me out of the room but instead gave encouragement and direction. And when I have slumped into "why bother?" thinking and feelings, I remember my own bravery and the kindness of others."

Another writer pitched his book to his ideal publisher and was rejected. Afterward, he realized he had pitched the book he thought would be accepted rather than the one he wanted to write. He revised his pitch and sent the publisher the new proposal. Her response? "This is the book we were hoping you had in mind." I often apply for grants way above my head because it's good practice; I figure by the time I qualify, I'll also have the grant-writing skills under my belt. For years I avoided social media, rebelling against the pressure to "have a platform"; once I made an author Facebook page, I used it grudgingly. Then I realized I could consider my page a place where writers of spiritual memoir could find the resources they need. Now I genuinely enjoy using that tool.

During the release our "drafts" are test runs, forays into new ways of being in relationship, sharing work, becoming a public

For me writing is an act of obedience ... I think about completed work and the submission process as part of the entire discipline of writing. I want to support journals, publications, and fellow writers—and I like to think I am honoring writing community . . . when I participate by submitting, reading, and responding. It wouldn't be accurate to say I don't celebrate publication success—it's probably better to say it's not my central intention, or not something I want to become central. My relationship with completed work looks something like: submitting it while writing other work, and then the new work becomes the work I am submitting, while writing more new work. Then, feeling blocked or like I'm not writing much, and revising old work. So I hold on to completed work in the interest of renewal! Maybe a good analogy would be training for a marathon. Even if one ends up not being able to participate in the intended race, the practice of regular exercise benefits the body.

—Lauren Carlson

presence, and bearing artistic responsibility. Test runs are how we learn to distinguish between resistance that's a natural part of transformation and resistance that signals we should stop. When do we hit a wall? When does a task start to feel icky? When do we cease learning and growing? Just as we learned how to slop down a draft, we new releasers must hazard a sloppy first step.

Unfortunately, our errors now involve other people. The stakes feel (and sometimes are) high. Consideration of others is a needful, tempering measure. Can we learn from and build on our mistakes regardless?

The only way forward is trial and error. Better to try, fail, and learn than be immobilized. You can always start small: a series of blog posts before a print publication, a $5 Facebook boost before an ad campaign. Movement, remember, is key. Learning through failure still moves the gift.

- Consider the next item on your to-do list. Imagine this task as part of a dialogue: By doing it, you put out a call. The universe will respond with information that may or may not be about your writing. How will you understand this answer? What will you do with it? How will you continue the conversation?

- After a task brings some result, ask yourself: What is my internal response to this outcome? What might be a life-giving response? How might I support the gift's movement? For instance, upon receiving a rejection you might pause to congratulate yourself for trying and resubmit the manuscript; upon receiving a critical review you might first tend the emotional wounds it inflicts before giving your book to a reader you know will appreciate it.

28 Form Community...

... With Those You Know

The other day, I had lunch with my poet friend, Christine. As a true extrovert, she began our time together by reading a draft of her latest poem, addressed to her daughter's birth mother. Our conversation then centered on the intimate, emotionally complex ways we adoptive mothers are bound to our daughters' biological mothers. The gift of her poem moved into our friendship.

I, on the other hand, an introvert and composer of long prose, am more likely to share with Christine the questions my writing raises and the insights I've gleaned. In the case of one-on-one relationships, the text of a project isn't necessary to keep the gift moving, but intention is. When Christine and I make plans for tea, we both anticipate our conversation. Christine makes a list. I mentally dig through what's happening in my writing life for a nugget or question. If I don't, the whims of conversation take over. Deliberation is key for passing the spark of our creative process into spoken words and actions.

"It is the cardinal difference between gift and commodity exchange that a gift establishes a feeling-bond between two people," Lewis Hyde writes. But even commercial transactions can convey gifts; consider a quick repartee with a cashier or the car mechanic you've trusted for decades. Whenever a relationship is formed or deepened because of your writing, the gift moves.

- Return to the mind map you created on page 112. Consider how people within the inner ring, those you know who embody your audience, have bestowed you with gifts. What have they contributed to your life? To this project? What is the nature of your relationship? What is the reciprocity between you?

- Brainstorm ways you might bring the gifts you've received through writing to these relationships—in conversations, in sharing the manuscript or printed copy, in attributions, through invitations to celebrate. Even if you intend to publish, this is an important step. Moving the gift in arenas where you're more apt to see results teaches you about its nature.

- How would sharing your project with these people today feel? What purposes might this serve? What would be your intention?

Keep in mind that most family and friends are notoriously bad readers. Emotional investment (in you or in your project's outcomes) invariably colors their reactions. Writers are inept at recognizing our motivations for sharing with those we love. We risk becoming victims of others' insecurities and need for control. Sometimes this risk is worthwhile, others not. Be slow and discerning.

... With Readers

Thirty years ago, I moved away from my beloved church community and agreed to keep in touch by writing a column for their newsletter. When I moved back, I continued the column because, unlike the memoir that was taking me a decade to write, people actually read it, discussed it, took issue with what I said, and thanked me. The column enriched our connections. It taught me how my words operate in the hearts and minds of readers.

Eventually the column morphed into a blog. I've faithfully composed these monthly reflections for decades because of the relationships they foster. Unlike the essays I publish in literary magazines, which always seem sucked into the ether, or online pieces, which ignite flash-in-the-pan reactions before vanishing, or even my books which, beyond sales figures and quick compliments, grant me little evidence of mattering, my blog instigates invigorating conversations and keeps me grounded in an obvious but easy-to-forget truth: Readers are real people. They are not "an audience." The abstract, generic, amorphous sense of audience is as detrimental to writers during the launch as it is during composition. Any consideration of broad groups of readers begins rightly with the particulars of one individual.

- Write a character sketch of your ideal reader. Why is this person up at midnight frantically turning your pages? What experiences brought them to this place? How will they feel once they set your pages down? What will they ponder? Now consider the real people you know, yourself included, who comprise this ideal reader. What more do they reveal?

- Have a conversation with someone who thoroughly appreciated your work. Who are they? Why did they read it? How did they experience your words? Try to detect the unique way your project now inhabits that person.

. . . With People in the Publishing Industry

Writers who work with publishers find themselves in a challenging power dynamic. We desperately want what agents and editors can bestow. They inhabit a seemingly elite literary domain to which many of us desire access. As a result, we project onto them (and the authors they represent) our own authority, power, and worth. Like therapeutic or professional relationships that include power imbalance and transference, these relationships are fertile ground for abuse. Writers are vulnerable. We must exercise caution.

Take, for example, publishers' simple request that writers not submit their manuscripts simultaneously to multiple journals. Journals can take up to twelve months to reject or accept a story. If writers average a dozen or two rejections before an acceptance, this request can pose an insurmountable barrier.

Or consider how often writers who receive an advance on their next book (with its corresponding deadlines) experience writer's block or produce mediocre work. The leveraging of money and expectation against the writing process, which by nature needs to be free, often winds up a form of servitude. The bravest writer I've ever met is a novelist who reneged on a book contract with a major publisher when she realized it was killing her soul. She walked away from an $800,000, two-book deal, eventually lost her agent, struggled to make ends meet for years, and had difficulty finding her next publisher. "I don't ever regret making that choice even though it truly torched my writing career," she wrote to me. "I'll never compromise my inner guiding voice and I know how to handle the pressures of corporate publishing so much better now (e.g., I would *never* sell a book before it's written, and I would make sure that if a publisher wanted to buy my book, they would have to accept my vision, purchase that vision, and not aim to change it)." Two decades later, she finally landed an agent and publisher who support her. She couldn't be happier.

When you present your writing to literary brokers early in your career, their power resides in money and influence while yours resides in your originality—your ideas, craft, voice, and product, all of which is and is not your doing. Yours is a hidden power flowing in an underground river. Lovely as this is, navigating the world of contracts, money exchange, and publicity is consequently challenging. The gift economy rarely interfaces smoothly with the market economy. How can you stand solidly beside your work in this gritty, rough-and-tumble business?

First, remember that editors, agents, and publishers are human. They may be caught up in corporate machinations but they still have dreams, moods, shortcomings, and talents. They genuinely want to discover good writing. They also want (or need) to make money. They are plowed under by submissions and must read stacks of manuscripts under pressure. While there are exceptions, generally the people who've gone into publishing love literature and want to support its creation and circulation. Often they are writers.

When you submit your writing along traditional channels, have compassion for the people at the other end. They wield power but that power comes with great cost. Consider the delicacy required to empathize with authors, respect their voices, and be invested in their happiness while also retaining critical distance, protecting the publisher, and asserting professional expertise, especially when its unwelcomed; consider the additional competing demands from the editing staff, designers, marketers, freelancers, and distributor. An editor's job is stressful.

Rather than thinking of soliciting an agent or publisher as "trying to sell your work," think of it like dating. You're looking for a good match. Sometimes the match is between the writing and the publisher; in the best circumstances, it's also between the author and the publisher. Either way you must come to know one another, get a sense of each other's personality and vision and working style, and see if you're compatible. Show up fully. Stay present, even when others can't or don't.

At first, this means doing research. As much as possible, look to the insides (the content and its presentation) rather than the outsides (the reputation, the money, the influence) of the journal or self-publisher or agency or publishing house. What is their guiding philosophy, their aesthetic, their mission? What else have they published? Why and how might you imagine them presenting your writing? Who is the particular person you're addressing? What about this person or their work makes you think they might augment your project's gift? If someone is interested in acquiring your project, ask them how they'd describe it to their best friend. Does their description match your understanding? Do you like how they talk about it? Is there chemistry between you? The agent or editor or publicist should sense this energy as well; "I need to feel that I am able to tell the story of the book with original and authentic passion," shares public relations professional Michael Taeckens in Tess Taylor's "The Art of Publicity." "Creating buzz happens through hard work, but I'm not performing magic tricks. I'm sharing my enthusiasm and I'm building relationships between authors and gatekeepers and also, eventually, readers." Only genuine connections lend integrity to our business dealings.

This requires writers to own our strength. I know, the power to turn down a publisher when you desperately want to see your work in print seems weak indeed, but this is the power of authenticity, of holding fast to values, of seeking what's real and lasting. Use it. As hard as it is to say no, and as painful as it is to receive a rejection, you can't deny that if one party has misgivings or isn't fully invested, the match isn't good. What you want is a healthy, enduring relationship.

The same principles apply to marketing. In Taylor's article, she describes how social media, instead of being a means of connecting with readers, had become for her "a distracting workspace where everyone clamors to be seen"—a common complaint of authors trying to promote our work. Publicity guru Lauren Cerand encouraged her to step back. "Social media can be a lonely place," Cerand advised. "You might be wiser building really key human relationships, with editors and other writers and readers, things that are more solid and less ephemeral." Taylor interpreted this to mean, "Slow down and gather real community in real life." Networking need not be a manipulative leveraging of others to your advantage, but rather the cultivation of bonds that offer mutual sustenance. Taylor writes, "The best 'networks' are really made out of only acts of deep humanity."

- Return to the mind map on page 112. Consider the people in your outer rings—those you are aware of but don't know, and others you're not yet aware of. How might you meet these people? What might a mutual relationship look like? Can your project facilitate this relationship?

. . . With the Writing Community

When I first conceded and jumped onto social media, I hired a coach. Her guiding advice was "Be a good internet citizen." Until then I'd never considered the internet a community gathering place. Now that's the primary way I try to relate online.

When you share your writing, you become a literary citizen. What kind of citizen will you be? Will you be generous and confident, doing the literary equivalents of shoveling the sidewalk, voting, contacting legislators, and volunteering? Or will you be needy, wanting attention and sales? What principles will guide your participation?

Sometimes we're inclined to engineer relationships to benefit our projects. Don't. Form connections for their own sake. Every person is a manifestation of the divine; when

"Think about publicity as something that connects you. Try to be as tender about publicity as you have been about making the work—put the work into the world as lovingly as you made it."

—LAUREN CERAND, IN
"THE ART OF PUBLICITY" BY TESS TAYLOR

we enter into relationship with another, we encounter a singular aspect of the sacred substantiated in that person. This is an end in itself. Healthy relationships are always reciprocal. Show up for others as well as asking them to support you. Collaborate. Remember that the community we build during the release is itself the gift moving in a new dimension.

- Transitioning away from a manipulative, self-centered stance toward the writing community isn't easy. Old patterns die hard. I'm reminded of a "Polish and Protocol" class I took in college in which we learned to look interviewers in the eye and offer a firm handshake. The "fake it till you make it" method works; it's a form of practice. Take note when you want those you meet to buy your book, acknowledge you as a serious writer, write a review, or otherwise serve your ego. Practice setting this want aside.

- Initiate mutuality. Seek your peers. Find an accountability buddy. Participate in a writing group, a poetry slam, a grant review committee. Review or blurb other authors. Give time and attention to newer writers who request help. Do for others what you would have them do for you.

29 Face the Inevitable Obstacles

When I was an exhausted new mom with a blitzed brain and zero solitude, I read an article by a writer-dad confessing that before kids he frittered away his hours at the keyboard, whereas now, with so little time, he wrote more effectively and efficiently. Obstacles magnified his creativity. Honestly, he pissed me off. So did my spiritual director, who said, "Maybe these are exactly the conditions you need to do your best work." A few years later, still juggling parenthood, money-making, and writing but with a full night's sleep, I noticed that whatever snatches of time I could nab unleashed in me a fierce and focused effort. People say, "If you want something done, ask a busy person" for a reason.

Paradoxical as it seems, most obstacles standing in the way of a writer launching a first (or second or third) work can contribute to the gift's movement. Just as internal resistance during the writing process often signals material worthy of attention, external obstacles often point to arenas worthy of our effort. When a client of mine wrote a memoir about losing her mother to cancer, she knew no press would publish it and didn't have the funds for self-publishing, so she tried crowd-funding the project. Hundreds of people who loved her mother contributed, giving her both the needed resources and a guaranteed readership. When mainstream publishers were unreceptive to my first book, determination helped me find a small but trustworthy religious press; I learned to weather rejection and adjust my expectations. Up to a point, impediments foster holy longing, encourage innovative thinking, and provide

There are, it seems, two muses: the Muse of Inspiration, who gives us inarticulate visions and desires, and the Muse of Realization, who returns again and again to say "It is yet more difficult than you thought." This is the muse of form. It may be then that form serves us best when it works as an obstruction, to baffle us and deflect our intended course. It may be that when we no longer know what to do, we have come to our real work and when we no longer know which way to go, we have begun our real journey. The mind that is not baffled is not employed. The impeded stream is the one that sings.

—WENDELL BERRY,
STANDING BY WORDS

the friction needed to spur us along. Like strict poetic form, limitations urge us toward inventive solutions.

What if my spiritual director was right and the external forces that stand in our way are in fact exactly right for the work we're called to do? I've never known extreme hardship, so I'm unqualified to answer this question. I do know that suffering (loss, depression, illness, insomnia) has brought me to my knees, where I have finally, humbly, allowed myself to be changed. Buddhist author Stephen Levine is often quoted as saying, "True healing happens when we go into our pain so deeply that we see it, not just as our pain, but everyone's pain. It is immensely moving and supportive to discover that my pain is not private to me." Every impediment or struggle invites us into communion with humanity. The gift's movement rarely takes the form we want or expect, but it can continue, if only in the transformation of our hearts. Perhaps this is precisely its purpose .

This does not mean we can be complacent. Real forces hamper our efforts: discrimination, the demands of family, financial limitations, time constraints, stiff competition, capitalism, health crises. . . . Roadblocks do rear up between our intention and the gift's movement. Some—poverty, systemic oppression, debilitating illness—can be insurmountable. Writers are censured, threatened, and imprisoned in many countries.   For writers everywhere, writing and publishing result in financial hardship.   Dominant U.S. culture privileges certain voices, forms, and narratives at the expense of others. People of color are under- and misrepresented in print.   Genre fiction will always garner more income than poetry.   Women's and nonbinary people's voices are rarer than men's on opinion pages, in review journals, and on bookshelves.   Queer writers remain pigeon-holed.

We should always rail against injustice, sweat in our effort to uplift human dignity, and tend individual and collective wellness.   But we can walk a middle path that neither dilutes our creative passion nor denies harsh realities but rather holds both in tension.   I lean on James Baldwin's *Notes of a Native Son* for guidance:

> It began to seem that one would have to hold in the mind forever two ideas which seemed to be in opposition.   The first idea was acceptance, the acceptance totally without rancor, of life as it is, and men as they are: in the light of this idea, it goes without saying that injustice is a commonplace.   But this did not mean that one could be complacent, for the second idea was of equal power: that one must never, in one's own life, accept these injustices as commonplace but must fight them with all one's strength.

Each of us is given, at any point in time, a unique set of circumstances.   Within these boundaries we do what we can with as much grace and peace as we can, while also fighting to change those boundaries.

Ultimately the gift's movement is a mystery.   It's not our doing.   In the face of obstacles, the practice of keeping our hearts open is an exercise of faith.

30 Embrace Brokenness

If you can't find a literary journal for your short story, is this because of its shortcomings, errors in your outreach, a traffic jam on an editor's commute downtown, or systemic injustice? When your aunt gives you the cold shoulder after reading your poem, is this rift your fault or a signal of her emotional hang-ups or a repetition of a family pattern? How do you make sense of the thrill of a publisher offering you a contract followed by heartbreak when they go bankrupt? Readers give authors tremendous authority, sometimes holding us accountable in important ways and sometimes projecting on us their own power, frustration, and responsibility. How do we know the difference?

Up until the release we've only dealt with private messiness, in our being and on the page. But during the release, our mistakes and shortcomings come into contact with the great brokenness of the world. We're all perfectly, wretchedly, human. Clear intentions get muddied. Pure hopes get dashed. We lose our way.

Lashing out at ourselves, our writing, or others is counterproductive. We can't control others or fix outcomes. Rather than spiraling into shame or blame, can we respond with love and creativity? Can we take responsibility for our part? The gift moves when each of us brings a full heart to whatever is. Compassion toward ourselves in difficult circumstances quickly morphs into compassion toward others.

When you find yourself in a mess, consider these questions.

- Christianity's early African monastics considered brokenness a given, a basic fact of humanity. Rather than berating themselves for wrongdoings, the desert mothers and fathers understood failings to be blessings because they are reliable gateways to spiritual growth. For Gregory of Nyssa, sin isn't wrongdoing; it's what happens when we refuse to grow. What are your broken places in this dilemma? How are they inviting you to grow?

- What brokenness in the wider world does the release help you recognize? Now that you see it, what difference does it make? How will you relate to it?

- Brokenness is a common human denominator. We all fall short of perfection. How might this current experience of failure, weakness, or limitations invite you to greater compassion?

- What is the scope of your agency? What are the limits beyond which you have no control? Hold yourself responsible only for your own words and actions. In what ways can your thoughts, effort, and creativity actively participate in moving the gift?

31   Think Currency

After my novel hit the bookstore shelves, the invitations to attend book groups began arriving. I was delighted. Wasn't being in conversation with readers what I most wanted? They offered me free publicity at a critical moment. I could support readers and strengthen our literary community. I was so grateful others were reading my book, I responded generously. . . .

Until I found myself driving long distances to suburban houses, listening to censored praise, answering questions like "How long did this take to write?", and then festering with resentment on the dark drive home. Introvert that I am, the social demands exhausted me. Despite my request that participants review the book online in exchange for my time, none did. The groups' presumption that I somehow benefited financially by attending enraged me. In an effort to make these visits worthwhile, I prepared questions I was curious to hear them discuss. Arriving, I grabbed the facilitation reins. Sure, conversations were then meaningful, but afterward I couldn't help calculating the money I should have earned for their orchestration. Eventually I quit saying yes.

I share this by way of saying that sometimes we offer time or goods freely and the gift does not move. In this case, I misjudged my place of abundance. The book groups, while well-intentioned, were unable to receive the full value of my gift. Despite there being no exchange of money, the evenings felt transactional. Whether due to my social reticence or mutual unrealistic, unmet expectations, no relationships formed. The spark I was so eager to share, that they were eager to discuss, dwindled in my presence.

I have a folder of free downloads on my computer (mostly resources about publishing) that I've never read. Their authors are stellar, their contents come recommended, and yet I never seem to make the time. Despite everything I know about gift economy, I nonetheless devalue what I haven't bought. From freelance teaching, I've learned that offering a class for free is a sure way for it to flop. Students leap to sign up but then don't attend.

The gift economy sputters in the face of hard-core social conditioning.

Let's look at the flip-side, how the market can aid the gift's movement. When I charge for a class, students' enrollment elicits commitment, willingness, and effort. Money exchange makes way for the gift's transmission.

When I turned twenty-three, my full-time job (teaching seventh grade English) meant that, for the first time, I had expendable income. On Friday evenings at our neighborhood bookstore, I treated myself to an impulse buy and strolled down to the lake to read. That's how I discovered Jetta Carleton's *The Moonflower Vine*. As I entered the steam and verdancy of Mary Jo's Missouri between that book's covers, my week of distractible preadolescents and even the shimmering south Minneapolis lake fell away. My life dissolved entirely until I surfaced again, straining to see the print in the descending darkness. Thirty years later I'm still blessed by the animated soul of Carleton's novel—its gift, sweetened by my own memory of youthful financial liberty and solitude by a city lake. Every spring now I plant moonflowers to admire with my daughter at dusk.

But back on the bookshop shelf, that softcover was pure commercial product. The gift jumped off the springboard of commodity exchange, from Carleton's imagination to my own to our garden to my daughter. To thrive as we navigate the marketplace, we need to stay focused on the gift. Is it moving? Does it have currency?

We live in a world that woefully under-compensates art-making as well as spiritual care, child-rearing, community-building, the healing arts, social justice efforts, environmental stewardship, and education. Artistic, spiritual, and relational endeavors are rendered invisible by the market economy and therefore collectively undervalued. They are often considered insubstantial, foolish even. Without adequate pay, many writers struggle to keep their spirits up and make ends meet. More never start.

How do we stay true to our creative spirit in this hostile environment? Sometimes writers *want* money and sometimes we *need* money, especially when our creative investment results in financial hardship. How do we tend the gift *and* keep a roof over our heads?

The task of shepherding gifts from internal to material realms, where they intersect with the market economy, then back into the subtle fabric of relationships, is neither easy nor simple.

Lewis Hyde recommends creating within a "gift-sphere," what I call a cloud of privacy, only "turning to see if it has currency in that other economy" once the work is faithfully realized. While this is ideal in principle, on the ground the intersection between gift and market economies is uniquely personal. Some authors, like my friend who reneged on her contract, refuse to accept a publisher's advance to avoid being beholden to anyone other than the Muse, despite the consequent financial hardship; some can't afford to dedicate time to writing without a grant, residency, or advance; and still others are motivated by pitching pieces and writing under contract. Some authors refuse to visit book clubs without compensation while others leap at the chance. There's no objective "right."

We each have an inner compass. As we wend our way through money brambles, our spiritual practice is to trust that steady needle, turning it always toward the gift.

Here are a few brambles in our path:

Gifts refuse to be quantified. We can't calculate the difference between a meal cooked with affection and one that isn't, between a hospital room cleaned with care and one cleaned for the paycheck, or between a treasured manuscript preserved in an attic and a book cranked out to garner kudos at the top of the best seller list. Those things we treasure most resist measurement.

When labor that moves a gift *does* receive compensation, there's always a disconnect between monetary value and real value. What is adequate pay for teaching a child to read? For planting a tree that lives a thousand years? For healing someone who's ill? For writing an article that gives a single reader, or thousands, hope? While monetary value and real value are not mutually exclusive, one is not the measure of the other.

When artists are paid for our labor, is the money deserved? We believe so. But can we tease apart the contributions of our own willful exertion from the faint breath of the Muse or the strong shoulders of our literary forebearers or our team of cheerleaders, babysitters, beta readers, and mentors? What exactly is being compensated— skill, popularity, wisdom, effort,

Money helps, to be sure. But if money were the only thing people needed in order to live creative lives, then the mega-rich would be the most imaginative, generative, and original thinkers among us, and they simply are not. The essential ingredients for creativity remain exactly the same for everybody: courage, enchantment, permission, persistence, trust—and those elements are universally accessible. Which does not mean that creative living is always easy; it merely means that creative living is always possible.

—ELIZABETH GILBERT,
BIG MAGIC

originality, "platform," good timing?   What's an appropriate amount?

Protecting parts of our social, cultural, and spiritual lives from the marketplace is critical to our well-being. Inspiration should never have a price tag, nor should love, clean water, or prayer. We need—for the sake of our souls—to honor and serve such gifts. They remind us of our dependence on one another and the earth. They connect us to mystery.

On the other hand, our capitalist milieu bends this sacred mandate to its will. New writers are expected to publish their work in exchange for a few copies, published authors are expected to speak at events, give readings, teach, and attend book groups without compensation "because it's good publicity," and marginalized writers are expected to donate their work for the sake of diversity and exposure. Artists are misused; our art is taken for granted.

Writing and its consequent obligations are *work*. Work should reap reward.

Money colors an audience's relationship to art. While a book's price tag or a literary journal's paywall means purchasers are more apt to read, the market value sets up expectations. We anticipate a return on our investment, a tit-for-tat exchange. The money we pay up front tends to diminish the agency of our gratitude on finishing. When we fork out money to buy *The New York Times,* we expect high quality reporting; we rarely feel grateful for it. The reporter and publication must make good on our investment, paying off the purchaser's debt with a gratifying experience. The reader doesn't finish with a sense of obligation to pay it forward. Sure, we might recommend a good article to friends but generally our gratitude is incorporeal and fleeting.

From this cultural milieu it's only a short leap for writers to judge their work according to status or monetary success. How many times have you met someone new, mentioned that you're a writer, and been smacked with the classic question, "Are you published?" Answer yes and you're revered; answer no and you're dismissed. When status is so blithely assessed, how can we not be affected?

An essential way to leverage social and economic change is to grow in awareness of the ways we've bought into this system—how we unconsciously esteem activities and products that receive monetary reward and denigrate those that don't—and shift our behavior. As novelist Janice Lee put it, "If I want to heal, if I truly seek freedom, it means that I have to free myself from the capitalist system of validation that I have been trained all of my life to participate in." Each private choice has public ramifications. Our every decision affects the whole. When we bring consciousness to these choices, considering not only ourselves and our readers but also the communities and systems in which we participate, we help shift our communities' misunderstanding and mistreatment of artists. The release is a chance to exert our influence.

Charles Eisenstein strives for "right livelihood" as he makes his decisions, such that "time, energy, and other gifts [go] toward something that enhances, preserves, or restores some aspect of the commonwealth, and the money (or other return gift) that comes in return does not require for its providence harm to nature and people." He convinced his publisher to accept a creative commons copyright, permitting readers to freely photocopy and share his material for any noncommercial purpose. "I see myself as a steward and channel for the ideas of *Sacred Economics.* . . . That is why I cannot, in good conscience, consider myself the morally legitimate owner of these ideas."

Eisenstein is a man with racial and gender privilege, professional clout, and enough financial resources to persuade his publishers to use recycled paper and accept a risky copyright status. Most of us don't have these advantages. In terms of our internal lives, however, this matters not a whit. We, too, can direct our choices according to love and reverence for the gift rather than a desire to maximize returns. Our sphere of influence may be small, we may make concessions to the market in order to pay the bills, and nonetheless we can each live into our own "right livelihood"; we can orient ourselves toward a higher purpose that includes both basic needs and our desire to give.

What feels good and right? For me, it's feeding my family, having enough but not too much, and being generous. What leads toward freedom, abundance, and trust? That's where true wealth lies.

Money transactions tend to disrupt relational bonds. Once everyone can hop in a car to buy a cup of sugar, there's no need to knock on a neighbor's door. In an environment reliant on money and its purchase power, people are less inclined to ask for help, be vulnerable, or count on others—all necessary elements for healthy relationships. If you want to find vibrant gift economies, look in traditional villages, neighborhoods with strong cultural or historical connections, and large immigrant families. The most interdependent neighborhoods are poor or working class, while the ultrarich don't even *have* neighbors. Gifts establish relational bonds between people; the sale of a commodity can but frequently doesn't.

Here are some guidelines that help me prioritize relationships while dealing with money matters:

- **Refuse to be exploited.** Proceed with dignity. Ask for fair compensation, especially if the project feels like a job or you need the money or you're negotiating with a wealthy organization. If all writers did this, we'd participate in a form of collective bargaining and change how the culture values art-making.

- **Don't exploit the gift.** Remember that you are its steward, not its originator nor its sole recipient. Keep your sights trained on increasing and moving the gift. The gift may appear temporarily as financial compensation but never equate the two.

- **Be generous from your abundance.** Give copies away as thank-you presents. Share your work orally. If you're able to donate profits to a charitable cause, this is an excellent way to separate money from creativity. Offer your time to individuals and organizations. Consider how your gift might help repair racial and economic disparities. Any way you can invest in the gift economy helps bolster it for everyone.

In an ideal world, we would have a robust gift economy where the circles of exchange are so far-reaching and generous we'd receive and give in balance. Everyone would have food, shelter, clothing, education, health care, clean water, and access to natural spaces. Everyone's presence and labor would be treasured. We can create this world; we should, as much as possible try. In the meantime, however, we function in broken systems. The best we can do is steer ourselves toward this second economy, giving when we're able, receiving when opportunities arise, generating pockets of exchange in our relationships and communities that play out our principles.

Money is one form of currency. The origin of the word *currency* is the Latin verb *currens*, or "moving." The flow of resources in watersheds, between plants and animals in a forest, or between the earth and its atmosphere is nature's wealth. Likewise, we're truly rich when our resources flow. In Genevieve Vaughan's *Women and the Gift Economy*, Jeannette Armstrong, a Syilx (Okanagan) from British Columbia, tells the story of her people's winter dance during which her mother gave away all her possessions. "If we don't know how to give like that, we are poor," she says. People who give with strings attached are described by the Syilx with a word meaning "swallower or destroyer of giving." I share Armstrong's example not to suggest giving away our work but rather to highlight the gift economy's alternative ethics. Wealth for the Syilx is defined by generosity. The current is key.

When money's movement supports the movement of a project's life-spark, it serves a good purpose. Focus on the movement.

If concerns about money interject themselves into your creative process or if launching your work stifles rather than uplifts your well-being, note the interruption of flow. Take time to reflect on the interconnections between creativity and money before proceeding.

- We all have needs. What in your desire for compensation is born of need? At what point will your needs be filled? In what ways are these needs holy and honorable? How might you participate in the market economy with dignity, integrity, and clarity?

- Just because we have needs doesn't mean we can't be deliberate. What do you have agency over? With clear intention, can you exert your energy toward those activities? What don't you have agency over? What outcomes *can't* you control? Can you practice letting these go?

- Sometimes we want what money symbolizes (status, respect, endorsement, connection, participation in a wider conversation, security) more than the money itself. What does money represent for you? What of your desire for compensation is need and what is want? What is the history of this desire? What is its relationship to your writing? At what point will your desire be satisfied? Does it have a sacred dimension?

- If you question your value as a writer or the value of your work because you're not compensated fairly, remember that true worth is never measured by remuneration. Pay attention to writing's currency. What other forms of compensation—joy in the creative process, personal growth, the sense of adventure, social rewards—can you identify? How might you better respect the worth of these intangible gifts?

- Remember that the gift moves from abundance. If money is scarce, what are other arenas of abundance from which you might give? If money is plentiful, how might you leverage money in service of the gift and others?

- Financial negotiations are often emotionally charged. Before you enter conversations about compensation, figure out a policy that's right for you and that fits each particular circumstance. Put it on paper. A written financial policy is easier to follow.

While money's currency has the unquestionable capacity to boost your writing's circulation and greater exposure can augment the gift's currency, this leap from one economy to the other crosses a hazardous canyon. Sure, in your effort to build bridges to readers you can print hundreds of copies or hire a publicist or buy advertising or create a fancy website; you can craft social media posts that share bits of the gift; pay for travel to engage directly with readers; make your online presence into a resource; form community around your newsletter—in other words, use best marketing practices. But under these bridges between writer and reader lurk the big bad trolls of greed, pride, and the forces of capitalism. Money itself guarantees nothing in the gift economy except danger. As soon as money flows, the threats to our own and the gift's wholeness increase.

The chasm between "making a living" and being an artist is the sad consequence of our collective economic values. There's no easy reconciliation. What we can do is turn our hearts toward that which we cherish. As much as each of us is able, according to our means and fortitude, we can launch work in ways that magnify the human spirit, nurture connections between people, generate trust, treat art and artists with dignity, and facilitate the circulation of gifts. In the wide spectrum of possibilities for how we do this, internal and external, material and immaterial, we each need to find what works for us, without judgment, then release the rest.

32   To Market, To Market

What a terrible irony, that after spending years working on a project, the first thing we have to do if we want to publish is write about what we've written! "The sincere reaction to making meaningful art is often speechlessness," Lan Samantha Chang tells us in her *Lit Hub* piece, "Writers, Protect Your Inner Life." "The finished product is like a pearl, complete and beautiful, but mute about itself." Chang quotes G.K. Chesterton, who said, "We have to speak of something of which it is the whole point that people do not speak of it; we have not merely to translate from a strange tongue or speech, but from a strange silence." It's a common complaint among artists, especially musicians and painters: If I could have explained what it's about, I wouldn't have made it!

Unfortunately, if writers want to share work through traditional means, remaining silent isn't an option.

Up until recently I assumed marketing meant trying to get people to buy a product. Advertisers spend money for the singular purpose of making money. I've marketed my books and found the work repugnant.

Then I was introduced to Mark Silver, a Sufi practitioner and business coach, who considers marketing a unique language. The purpose of this language is not to sell a product or service but rather to move the gift. "If you use marketing syntax, your marketing becomes the same as delivering your product or service," he teaches. Marketing syntax gives away the essence of your gift. "The power of marketing syntax allows people to taste the value of what you are offering before they ever buy anything." I now consider every Facebook ad and book description a chance to giftwrap and freely offer some portion of what I've received.

Silver's use of linguistic metaphors helped me reframe marketing as a final step in the writing process—another revision into a radically new form. What a paradigm shift! With this perspective I see that I released five books without ever generating language that effectively offered their gifts. The words and images my publishers and I have used to package my books tried to sell a product; we never dug into the books for their essence and attempted to give it away.

What *is* marketing syntax for writers? According to Mark Silver, it is language that

1) sees the personhood of the reader without judgment;
2) addresses the reader's longings with empathy and care; and
3) becomes a catalyst for connection.

By way of example, here's a description of *Living Revision*:

> Creative writing brings you joy, yet when you're ready to take your draft to the next level you find yourself overwhelmed, losing momentum, and wanting direction. *Living Revision: A Writer's Craft as Spiritual Practice* helps you reconnect with the source of your inspiration to generate work that's heart-centered, artful, and effective.

And here's what I didn't write—but should have—for the novel:

> How can we move from fear into rich, risk-filled lives? This book tells a story of how inexplicable

passion, buried strength, and professional skill usher one woman into profound faith in life itself. Her body is her portal.

Identify and pitch your unique contribution to the larger conversation. In its most authentic form, this is what "branding" is.

—Reema Zaman in "How Entrepreneurs and Authors Can Amplify Their Powerful Voices," Forbes Magazine

Rather than publicize your project, marketing syntax directly moves the gift by offering it in part. Most significantly, marketing is about the reader—not about you, not even about your work. If we began writing with complete freedom, unrestrained in any way by audience, and if over revision we gradually welcomed audience into our process and craft, here at the release the subject of our creative effort *is* the audience. The centerpiece of heart-centered marketing is the audience who has emerged *through* you and your project.

Understood this way, marketing begins with listening. Who does your creative work address? What do those people care about? How do they describe themselves? Where within their being is the life-spark of your project already burning? This exercise of empathy is essential to the launch; it crafts the only path into relationship our creative work can travel.

- Return to the final exercise on page 113, where, having traced the life of your audience, you described their attributes and identified their longings, curiosity, passion, hurts, or questions—the "problem" your project addresses. Can you compose a single, compelling sentence that calls your audience by name, discusses their "problem" with empathy, and opens a conversation? Consider this the jumpstart for your marketing materials.

33 Receive the Blessings of Failure

There's an old Taoist story about a farmer whose horse ran away. On hearing this, his neighbors came to him and said, sympathetically, "Such bad luck!"

"Bad luck, good luck—who knows?" the farmer replied.

The next day the horse returned, bringing with it three other wild horses. "So wonderful!" the neighbors exclaimed.

"Bad luck, good luck—who knows?" the farmer said.

Then the farmer's son tried to ride one of the untamed horses, was thrown off, and broke his leg. The neighbors offered their sympathy for his misfortune.

"Bad luck, good luck—who knows?" the farmer said.

The day after that, military officials came to the village to draft young men into the army. Seeing that the son's leg was broken, they passed him by. The neighbors congratulated him on how well things had turned out.

You can guess the farmer's reply. Equanimity like this is born of resisting judgment and cultivating possibility. If we foster a worldview broad enough to see the blessings of failure and the dangers of success, we walk the middle way. For me, zooming out to see the bigger Story's evolution helps me attend what's coming alive, regardless of my small story's success or failure.

The release is a great chance to practice equanimity. Practice is the point.

- Quickly list experiences you've had writing or releasing writing into two columns—"successes" and "failures."

Then reflect: Why did you designate each item as you did? What were you seeking and did or didn't find such that you declare it a success or failure? What external standards help you determine what's successful or not? What internal ones? How might the items in one list just as easily fit into the other?

When you want to release work but can't (for whatever reason: it's been rejected, you're exhausted, the computer crashed, you're dealing with a family crisis or illness), you face "failure." But use caution around this word. *Failure* brands the work, the process, and the maker. When you think in terms of success and failure, your hope (and sometimes identity) is latched onto some result. And when that result is not what you wanted, it's easy to shutter your heart to a myriad other outcomes. Movement occurs where we least expect it.

When writers confess to me their fear of failing—of putting pen to page where they'll see their inadequacies, of not doing justice to their experiences or ideas, of rejection, of bad reviews—I respond gayly, "Of course you'll fail." I quote Margaret Atwood: Failure is just another name for much of real life. And while this is cause for distress, it's also a balm. "There may be no success like failure," Bob Dylan purportedly said, "but far from failure being no success at all, in its very visceral intensity, it is perhaps the only success there is."

This rings true for me. In the moment, each failure feels wretched. Embarrassed, grieving, bitter, I want to curl up in a hole. As I begin to massage the sore spots, though, eventually I recognize how my failures spawn my most cherished gifts. *The Release* is one example; I've hundreds more. After enduring two years of rejections from publishers, my first book was accepted by Skinner House, the Unitarian Universalist press. The print run was 750 copies. They had no distributor. Sure, I was happy to see my memoir in print, but I also secretly felt that the press—so small, so narrowly focused, so lacking in resources, so unable to market my book—was a sign of my failure. For years I dismissed Skinner House. I didn't offer them my second book, a collection of personal essays, but rather sought and found a good mid-list press. Eventually Skinner House asked me to write what became *Writing the Sacred Journey* and also published *Living Revision*; they kept *Swinging on the Garden Gate* in print for more than a decade, long after the mid-list press had been eaten up by a conglomerate and my essay collection remaindered; they reprinted *Swinging* in a second edition. Today I have a twenty-five-year working relationship with an editor I respect. I've become a proponent of small presses. Skinner House's endorsement of my little memoir has morphed into an immense, ongoing blessing.

Once I gave a reading about growing up bisexual and Christian to an audience at a large university. Because I neglected to distinguish my faith from the conservative Christianity that has condemned most LGBT folks, a trans woman lambasted me during the Q&A: "How *dare* you say I'm sinful?" I'd said nothing of the sort. Even so, I was horrified that I had caused her pain and that the event had been marred by angry shouting. After forcing myself to approach her, we talked through our misunderstanding and in the end embraced. I learned to carefully delineate my particular experience of Christianity and not shy away from conflict.

Writers' most common experience of failure during the release comes with rejection—from family or friends who dislike what we've written or, worse, refuse to read it; from agents and publishers; from reviewers who pan our work or, worse, ignore it. There's a plethora of advice in literary circles about how to deal with rejection, from wallpapering your office with rejection slips to rejecting the rejector to receiving each rejection as an invitation to work harder. I'm leery of any one-size-fits-all solution. Instead, I suggest three practices that cultivate equanimity.

1. **Accept that rejection is part of the publishing process.** Acquisition editors decline most of what they see, for many reasons other than quality—the press's priorities, duplication with other books in their list or articles in their journal, their particular market and branding, and their capacity to do the piece justice, to name a few. All published authors have received copious rejections. Don't take rejection personally; it likely has little to do with you or your writing. Detachment helps us step off the emotional rollercoaster of the submission process and instead see *what is*.

2. **Open yourself to the invitations of rejection.** "If handled properly, without knee-jerk chagrin or defensiveness, rejection can lift us beyond the childlike state of looking for approbation and allow us to see our work in a bigger sphere, from a multiplicity of perspectives," writes Grant Faulkner in "Rejection's Gift":

> We have to ask what's missing in a story or poem. We have to probe our work to see if it lives up to our vision. We have to question the vision itself. Are we willing to buck the opinion of others to realize our concept of a work? Do we compromise in order to find the acceptance, or does rejection illuminate another path altogether? Does rejection weaken us and make us buckle under its weight, or does it motivate us to go deeper into our work and push harder?

Rejection presents resistance; are you going to crumble or push back? The obstacle might be an industry biased against people of color, or a cultural climate unreceptive to your ideas, or a historic occurrence that usurps everyone's attention. Perhaps it's your false sense of grandiosity, your lack of knowledge about the press you've solicited, the limitations of your craft, or flaws in the project's content. Perhaps the slots on the publisher's list are full. Rejections accompanied by explanations are treasures because they initiate relationship and sometimes help you revise, but unfortunately few places send personalized rejections these days. We're left to ask ourselves, "Given the fact of *this* rejection, how will I not just react but respond creatively? With resolve? With a willingness to learn? With political action? With more labor?"

3. **Revisit the meanings of success and failure.** How does this rejection make you feel? Why? What's the history of these feelings? What do they expose about your need for approval or recognition? Your need for security or control? What do they reveal about how much or little you value the creative process? Every rejection is a chance to redirect your attention toward what matters most.

I believe that my choice, at this moment, to not pursue publication is a success, not a failure. I've dug really deep within myself to write the experience. I can let the public confession of it go, too. I still see myself growing as a writer and as a spiritual person as a result of having written it.

—MARY BERG

Rather than sentimentally "looking on the bright side," equanimity asks us to live into whatever opportunities arise in the charred remains of our dreams. The visceral intensity of failure—horror, embarrassment, shame, grief—may, over time and with deliberation, prove initiatory. We can emerge on the other side burned but better for it.

• Can you faithfully love and appreciate your creative work after others have rejected it? Without belittling or rejecting others in return? How can you express this affection concretely?

- A poverty of affirmation from others asks of us more profound trust in ourselves. What are you seeking externally and not receiving? How might you fill this need internally? What other ways might you fill it externally? What role does trust or faith play?

- In the onslaught of what you perceive as failure, what's coming alive? How can you respond creatively? How might you or your project grow?

34 Beware the Hazards of Success

We presume certain landmarks in a publishing career (getting a grant, attending a writers' colony, finding an agent, signing a contract, receiving a first review) are moments of arrival. "If only X would happen," we think, "I'll be golden." Janice Lee describes this as the "escape we are looking for," the "myths of meritocracy and the capitalist paradigms where legitimacy and success are so closely linked." The desire for recognition, as informal as a single reader's praise or as public as a Pulitzer, often lurks in writers' hearts.

But success as currently defined by the dominant U.S. culture has serious pitfalls, primary among them being that these myths cast "many of us as undeserving, mediocre, and invisible," as Lee points out. The myths steer us toward money and popularity. American readers exercise a strange form of hero worship, elevating authors to altitudes with little oxygen and projecting on authors their own better selves, thus exempting themselves from pursuing their own creative genius. The kudos a celebrated author receives can actually strip readers of their own authority and falsely idolize the celebrity. If we writers accept such warped praise, we bolster false egos all around.

When others reward us for our art, they attribute to our selfhood much that we can't lay claim to—the miracle of inspiration, the give-and-take of revision, the convergence of effort, luck, talent, privilege, timing, patience, and connections needed to publish—and leave us feeling fraudulent. Longing still pulls at our bones; we still hunger for creative practice; we (shockingly) remain our same-old inadequate selves. The disconnect between outer and inner realities is unsettling.

Writing for real people has real consequences. Readers' expectations can feel like pressure or responsibility. Time in the limelight can be exhausting, constraining. As wonderful as it is to hear others' positive responses, the uptick in communications is soon overwhelming. We imagine success will give us more time to write; almost always it gives us less.

Success tricks us into thinking we can rest on our laurels. The transformational journey is done. This foreclosure on possibility is success's grave danger: We stop growing.

Yes, we ought to be proud of our accomplishments. Genuine gratitude from readers, any evidence of lives transformed for the better, fertile dialogues or relationships that result from our writing—these successes are worth honoring. When you notice yourself deflecting others' gratitude or affection, pause. As Charles Eisenstein observes:

> One of the most important gifts you can give is to fully receive the gift of another . . . When someone pays me a compliment, I sometimes reject it by denying its truth, projecting false humility, or devaluing it with words like, "Oh, everybody does it; it's not so special." When someone says, "Thank you," sometimes I find myself rejecting it with words like, "It was nothing." Someone might say, "Your writing has changed my life," and I might respond, "The change was within you already, and my writing was merely its agent. Others read the same

words with no effect." While there is truth in this response, nonetheless I have sometimes used it to deflect gifts of praise or thanks that I was afraid to fully receive, to fully take in. Another way to reject the gift of a compliment is to pay a return compliment with excessive alacrity, distracting from the first compliment before it has a chance to sink in. When gratitude inspires a return gift, we must not give it too quickly, or it becomes a mere transaction, not so different from a purchase. Then it cancels out obligation rather than tying giver and receiver more closely. . . . Clearly then, reluctance to receive is actually reluctance to give.

Genuine gratitude and authentic love circulate the gift. They also call attention to the best expression of our gifts. Receive them.

Likewise, when others attribute authority to our work, we have a duty to bear that authority with intention. "We are responsible for the way the world appears before us, for its depth and richness (if we are open to others) or its poverty (if we are not), and for the impact our vision has on others," novelist Charles Johnson warns. What will you do with this newly granted influence? You can exercise humility, taking care not to pin your worth or identity on it. You can help forge what Janice Lee calls "another way," one more aware of how "we have all internalized publishing supremacy, the harm of unconsciously assigning more worth to books or authors that have had more commercial success, of using language that feeds the idea of linear progress and hierarchy." You can leverage your power in service—of causes dear to you, of others, of your principles. You can move the gift.

The small story may be finished but the big Story continues. External recognition is a good reason to exercise internal equanimity. How can you best serve the Story through or in spite of others' affirmation? What is yours to do?

The publication of my first book, *Swinging on the Garden Gate*, granted me a passport into places and communities previously inaccessible to me. I discussed Christianity with transgender folk, shared my story of coming out bisexual in more churches than I can count, was a visiting author at my high school, and was invited to speak at the Unitarian Universalists' General Assembly. Authors don't have to become their work's ambassadors—we can remain reclusive—but if we do travel outward we have the opportunity to encounter readers and be changed. Meeting my audience became for me a form of revision; I got to see my story (and through my story the bigger Story) through the lens of queer folks hurt by the church, elderly church ladies, and disinterested high schoolers. As a public voice, I grew more considerate, confident, and responsible.

With the circulation of a project, the writer's internal life participates in public discourse. One of my most gratifying writerly moments occurred during my MFA thesis defense, at which three authors and one theologian discussed my memoir for a good hour. The conversation wasn't about me; it focused on the work, the ideas, and the art. The experience was exhilarating and profoundly satisfying. Integrating into my manuscript the suggestions from that discussion took me a full year. One of the reasons I seek out traditional publishers for my work is that, in the best of circumstances, I partake in similarly generative conversations with agents and editors. This tempers my thinking and my prose. Audiences challenge me with alternative perspectives. Over time I've grown into the public role a writer plays—as storyteller, truth-teller, teacher, conversation-starter. I consider these gifts worthy compensation.

You can use your public engagements as an excuse to pat yourself on the back or you can accept them as fodder for transformation and service. What makes the difference is your intention. In the end, we're called not to succeed so much as to remain faithful to the path.

35   Welcome Emptiness

After having done my best to launch a book, I enter a no-man's-land, a sprawling, barren landscape I must crawl across to reach the oasis of my next project. Skulking just beyond the release is something every writer fears: emptiness. It's a loss like any other—sad, an end, but also an opportunity. If I accept the emptiness, traversing it willingly; if I mourn what I've lost, realize my inability to do much about it, and appreciate the gifts I've received, a lush spot usually glimmers on the horizon.

Gifts are given without strings attached. The hollowness we feel after the release is the space remaining after the gift moves on.

I think of post-launch emptiness as a counterpart to the blankness of the original page, like two vacuous bookends flanking the creative process. Thus concludes your active involvement with a project. This is not, however, the end of your intention, nor of your creativity, nor of your transformational path. Cross the emptiness with a full heart.

36 Release

Oddly, the primary mover and shaker during the release is the project itself—the essay, story, poem, or book. The more time passes, the less you can do. At some point, your ability to support the project ends. Perhaps you run out of energy or money or ideas; perhaps the project has had its day; perhaps the piece prospers without you, or within you. The baton is passed. The gift's locus is elsewhere. Your child is an adult—with a job, no less, and perhaps a family! Transformation happens at the crossroads between the project, others, and Mystery. You hover just behind your story's shoulder, but the bulk of your work is complete.

Once, after I'd suffered a disappointing romantic breakup, a friend reassured me that love is never wasted. Despite all evidence to the contrary, the love you've showered on your project matters. Love makes the entire creative process dialectical, relational—a conversation with others and with the creative Source. Love expands us; it "brings about an increase in being," as my teacher Cynthia Bourgeault says in *Love Is Stronger Than Death*, "and it does so by giving us the courage and power to live out of who we truly are." That increase is the whole point of creation. The love born of your writing (for the process, for the subject, for the craft, for the gifts) is itself the fruit.

We writers—we humans—long for creative fulfillment, which we've been taught to measure with public attention or commercial success. But true creative fulfillment is found in creating, and in the love born of creating. Perhaps that love is what we've most wanted all along.

Final Thoughts

Deep in the thickets of revising *Swinging on the Garden Gate*, I stumbled on what has become for me writing's most compelling mystery: creating creates us. What began with the ego-boosting notion—*I'm writing a book!*—waking me at dawn to write before commuting to my teaching job, eventually propelled me to come out bisexual, to be more forthright, to follow the stirrings of vocation into retreat ministry, to find my voice both on the page and in person, to discover an inherent wholeness binding together the disparate threads of my experiences. . . . That original egoic motivation instigated eight years of toil and radical personal transformation. Only gradually did I awaken to its illusion. Sure, I was writing a book, but the primary generative movement was in the opposite direction. *I* was the ultimate creation. My memoir ignited an explosion of becoming that continues to this day.

Stephen King puts it more plainly: "Life isn't a support system for art. It's the other way around." Our lives are expansive vessels, able to receive generativity's abundance. In the reciprocity of the creative process, who we become for having created is the gift wondrously increased. That original spark is forged into text, yes, and also passes into bone and blood, into being, into becoming. "If your life is burning well, poetry is just the ash," Leonard Cohen once said.

Let's not forget this principle fire.

I'd like to share one last story before closing. Darby Nelson, a retired Minnesota legislator and biology professor, showed up in my creative nonfiction class one day flashing a goofy smile, eager to write a book about how humans love our lakes to death. Over ten years, I supported him to write what eventually became *For Love of Lakes,* a personable dive into lake ecology published by Michigan State University Press. Darby was astonished by (and welcomed) the emotional challenges of revision; he thrived during the book's release, speaking at countless environmental conferences and lake association meetings across two states. In anticipation of his second book, Darby and his wife Geri paddled every inch and tributary of the Minnesota River, built a sweet writing studio in his yard, and spent years researching and conducting interviews. But partway through drafting *For Love of a River: The Minnesota,* Darby was diagnosed with dementia. He and Geri amped up the project's pace. Darby desperately wanted to complete this book before he lost his faculties.

As Darby's memory faded, every change to the manuscript agitated him. Geri took charge. From the sidelines, I wondered whether the couple's frantic activity—coordinating with a ghost writer, finding a self-publisher, editing, choosing a cover, putting out publicity—was really how they wanted to spend Darby's final cogent months. Darby delighted in canoeing, cross-country skiing, anything outdoors. They had kids, grandkids. Yes, the book was important, but was it *that* important? Especially when it could never be as elegant or impactful as *For Love of Lakes*?

Over two hundred people attended the release party, held at the University of Minnesota's Bell Museum in the fall of 2019. When I hugged Darby, Geri had to remind him of my name. His thank-you speech was short and stuttered. Everyone bought copies. Darby grinned madly the entire time, unable to follow conversation but nonetheless elated. The room was warm with affection. When he died a few years later, I thought back to that happy evening and saw what their labor had made possible: A gathering to celebrate the life's work of a man dedicated to Minnesota's waters; a culmination; less a book launch than a living memorial. Darby's life burned bright that evening. The book was the ash.

When I support a writer over years, I gain a privileged vantage from which I can witness a more magnificent but usually veiled "end product." It radiates from our personhood like Darby's smile. It strengthens our relational bonds. It reverberates through communities and, I believe, transcends time. Often invisible and intangible, this creation moves within, through, and beyond us. Darby and Geri transferred their book's gifts into strengthened relationships and, subtly, into Minnesota's collective care for our waters. Their effort was of utmost—I'd say eternal—value.

Just as a trauma healed impacts a genetic line, just as a tree planted today provides shade, shelter, and clean air for generations, and entangled particles at opposite ends of the universe remain strangely linked, the relationships born of a creative release bear fruit—within meaning and memory, identity and dreams, purpose and perspective; with our intimates, our home and place, our widening circles, and our sacred origins and ends. The gift is an "order added to the sum of the universe's order," to return to Annie Dillard's words. Your story, each of our stories, contributes to what Valentine Tomberg calls in *Meditations on the Tarot* the world's moral memory, "the book of life," where one finds "complete texts of manuscripts written by authors—who . . . entrusted them to the four winds, addressing them to anyone into whose hands they would perhaps at some time fall." The gifts matter.

Because quantum entanglement has become for me a reason for hope, bear with me while I linger there. When tiny particles like electrons or photons link, they act like a single entity. Even if separated by light years, when one spins clockwise three times, the other spins clockwise three times. Isn't that wild? To illustrate quantum entanglement, John Preskill, a professor of theoretical physics, uses—of all things—the analogy of reading. In his article "What Is Entanglement and Why Is It Important?" he explains that in the everyday world, which behaves according to classical mechanics, we read each word, sentence, and paragraph consecutively, gradually gleaning the book's content. But if a book is highly entangled, its information is stored in the correlations between its various components. Meaning is held in the matrix.

I believe both are true, that the meaning made in a Newtonian worldview coexists with meaning found in a quantum universe. We are like the characters in Ray Bradbury's *Fahrenheit 451*, human carriers of the stories we've read and stuff we've written, now in entangled form, their significance in its entirety stored in our being, the connections no longer "local," as physicists call the physical plane, but rather residing between particles synced and spinning on an infinitesimal scale. Gifts form connections within and between people; they entangle us. Or as science and theology scholar Ilia Delio writes in *Making All Things New*, "The magnitude of our relatedness is the breadth of our lives, and the degree to which we live on in the evolution of life. . . . After I am dead, my own self is woven into yours. 'I' am not just my atoms or my genes. . . . We live on in our relationships, and, in and through our relationships, we are continuously created." In a quantum world, this is simply what happens.

When writers (with astonishing frequency) tell me, "I don't want to die before finishing this project," their instincts are spot-on. Writing offers us immortality, but not in the way most of us assume. Publishing can't make a meaningless life meaningful. Reputation won't guarantee that we're remembered. A book on a shelf preserves our spirit only for a duration. No, the creative act itself lives in perpetuity by increasing the gift. We come more alive by writing; we grow more entangled. This consequent expansion of presence and relationship is what endures.

"Love the art in yourself, not yourself in the art," Russian actor Konstantin Stanislavski advises. Love the miraculous artistic creation already wrought within you; love the process of becoming that the art avails you; love how creating awakens and raises up the creator within. Love the project for the art it ushers into your living. The quickening that leapt from your being to the page and from the page back to your being is inimitable and unequaled. Had you blocked it, it would be forever lost. That you've birthed it is astonishing, an offering beyond measure. This ineffable generation of being, I've come to believe, is the only effective agent of change here on this sweet planet and our only lasting contribution to the cosmos.

Slowly, haltingly, I move from an *eros* love for writing, which seeks some benefit for myself, to an *agape* love, one which seeks the good of the beloved. For writers the beloved is the work itself, craft, content, and process; the beloved is the reader, both literal and eternal; the beloved is anything, really, we give ourselves to through the page. *Agape* goes out from myself and does not return because it's all gift. It seeks the welfare, the thriving, of the beloved. Wondrously, in the giving I receive tenfold. What is the gift economy other than the flourishing of reciprocal, self-giving love?

Composing these pages has helped me steer my little writing canoe away from ego gratification and the need to make a difference, toward writing as a means of loving. I hope this book has done the same for you.

Acknowledgments

These pages are peopled with countless writers—far more than I've named—who graciously shared with me the inner workings of their writing life. These seekers, amateur and professional alike, have shown me I'm not alone in cherishing the transformational dimension of writing. They've confirmed my intuitions that craft is a trustworthy framework for spiritual growth and taught me how to sustain creative practice beyond completion. I'm profoundly grateful to every student, client, colleague, and friend who's written alongside me over the past quarter century and helped form this book.

I credit my wisdom teachers for returning me to an abundant, joyful faith in creativity. This project is a direct outgrowth of two years in The Living School, an immersion in Christian mystical thought and practice hosted by the Center for Action and Contemplation in Albuquerque, New Mexico. There I sat at the feet of Richard Rohr, Cynthia Bourgeault, James Finley, and Ilia Delio, who introduced me to a lineage I now claim as my own. The Sisters of St. Joseph's Wisdom Ways Center for Spirituality then offered me space to apply contemplative principles to creative writing, and now The Eye of the Heart Center brings them forward in community-based practice. To the awesome spirit moving through these ministries, I offer my gratitude.

The following writers and readers have directly supported this project: Marcia Peck, Carolyn Crooke, Mark Powell, and Terri Whitman, my trustworthy, hardworking, wildly generous writing group; Carolyn Kolovitz, Beth Wright, Christine Sikorski, Mona Susan Power, Nancy Nordenson, Julie Neraas, Robert Glass, Mary Berg, Tom Bloom, Abby Bloom, Nancy Agneberg, Lenore Franzen, Liz Olds, Linda Varvel, Douglas Owens-Pike, Annegret Rice, Carolyn Holbrook, Lisa Bullard,

Charity Yoro, and Emily Jarrett Hughes, all of whom read drafts and offered invaluable thoughts; William Brock, Matt Mumber, Cheryl Conklin, Endal Kallas, Cindy Kroll Barke, and Dave Hall, who guided this project's early metaphysical formation; Laura Kelly Fanucci, Erika Alin, Paul Lutter, Lauren Carlson, Nancy Agneberg, Mary Berg, and many more who shared testimonials; Scott Edelstein and Beth Wright for their publishing advice; and Mary Benard, Pierce Alquist, and Skinner House who, much to my ongoing amazement, convey my words into readers' hands. To the village who raised both this book-child and its author, my heartfelt thanks.

A question my eight-year-old daughter asked incited this project. To Gwyn, to Emily who steadies me through the release's ups and downs, and to the Spirit of creation breathing in and through us all, I bow in gratitude.